W9-BUD-734

MINISTERING
TO THE DYING

SUCCESSFUL PASTORAL COUNSELING SERIES

MINISTERING

TO THE DYING

CARL J. SCHERZER

PRENTICE-HALL, INC., ENGLEWOOD CLIFFS, N.J.

Ministering to the Dying
by Carl J. Scherzer

T–58427

Prentice-Hall International, Inc.
(*London, Tokyo, Sydney, Paris*)
Prentice-Hall of Canada, Ltd.
Prentice-Hall de Mexico, S.A.

Printed in the United States of America

DEDICATION

To
Gretchen and Ron,
Joy and Bob,
Bill, Shari and Heidi.

Fear not, for I am with you,
 be not dismayed, for I am your God;
I will strengthen you, I will help you,
 I will uphold you with my victorious right hand.
 Isaiah 41:10

INTRODUCTION

This series of books represents the most comprehensive publishing effort ever made in the field of pastoral care. These books could not have been published twenty-five years ago, or probably even ten, for the material was not then available. In the past, single books have been available covering different phases of the task. Now we are bringing the subjects together in a single series. Here we present a library of pastoral care covering the major topics and problems that most pastors will encounter in their ministry. Fortunately, not all of these problems need be faced every week or even every month. But, when they are, the minister wants help and he wants it immediately.

These books are prepared for the nonspecialized minister serving the local church, where he is the most accessible professional person in the community. It is a well-accepted fact that more people turn to clergy when in trouble than to all other professional people. Therefore, the pastor must not fail them.

Russell L. Dicks
General Editor

PREFACE

One of the clergyman's most exacting and meaningful responsibilities is his ministry to the dying. As important as this phase of pastoral calling is, comparatively little has been written to offer guidance to the Protestant clergy, particularly those newly ordained.

The Roman Catholic Church has defined its ministry to the dying quite clearly, but Protestant and Jewish clergy must rely largely upon their own intelligence and the guidance of the Holy Spirit. While ministering to the dying calls for a high degree of the pastor's discipline and devotion, it is also rich in its blessings to him spiritually.

So much of our customs and thinking contradicts our beliefs in immortality that the pastor almost stands alone at the patient's bedside, with the exception of the Lord's Presence. When all else fails to prolong earthly life, the dying person looks to the clergyman as the only one who can offer guidance and comfort. Since he must minister to the spiritual needs of one whose next dawn will be the eternal day, no one can serve as a substitute for him at that time.

The similarities and differences in concepts regarding death and immortality must be considered in an adequate ministry to the dying. In all three major American religious philosophies there are definite assurances that man's destiny is eternal. There are, however, divergent opinions regarding the *nature* of the eternal life, punishment and reward. These opinions depend upon various concepts of God and His holy will for man.

It is commonly believed by churchmen that man's earthly life

9

is the preparation for the extension of it into the life eternal. Each individual is the earthly guardian of his own soul. God alone is the final Judge of man's merits. Therefore, no man should presume to judge his fellowman.

Through the inspiration of the Holy Spirit, man may be so guided in his way of life that he may confidently approach the threshold of death. It is the minister's responsibility to assist his people in finding spiritual fulfillment on earth so they may hopefully envision their inheritance through service and joy in the life to come. The eternal phase of man's being flows from the life here and now into eternity.

This book is not primarily intended as a handbook for clergymen, although the sections on reassurance are convenient for that purpose. Rather, it is written to bring into focus the spiritual resources that are available to help man feel at home in the Presence of God, now and forever.

Sincere appreciation is expressed to the following friends for their invaluable assistance: Russell L. Dicks, Father William Freeman, Rabbi Martin Douglas, Friedrich Rest, Grace and Albert Hahn, Sister Sophia Bartelt, Irma Bolte and Clara Zuspann. In addition, my deep gratitude is due many physicians, pastors, nurses, patients, and my wife, Virginia, who have shared this ministry with me.

C.J.S.

Books by Carl J. Scherzer

Meditations for the Sick
The Church and Healing
Springs of Living Water
Followers of the Way
Understanding Christianity
      (co-author with Dr. Edgar McKown)
Ministering to the Physically Sick

CONTENTS

MINISTERING
TO THE DYING

CHAPTER ONE

PHILOSOPHIES Of DEATH
And IMMORTALITY

In my student nurses' philosophy class I asked, "Why do you think so many people, both Christian and non-Christian, believe in some form of immortality?" Of the conjectures offered, one student responded, "I suppose it's because other people feel it as I do at times."

"Can you explain what you mean by 'feel'?" I asked.

"I can't explain it," she responded. "I just know that my soul is eternal because I feel it at times, especially when I pray."

According to the Genesis narrative, man was created very good (Gen. 1:31), that is, in harmony with God and nature and without sin. It can be implied from the statement, "for in the day that you eat of it you shall die" (Gen. 2:17),[1] that it was God's intention that man, as long as he lived in blessed harmony with God, would exist indefinitely in the body in which he was created.

However, many eminent theologians contend that this statement means that through disobedience man would experience an early death and not live eternally as the sole form of humanity on earth.[2]

"Then the Lord God said, 'Behold, the man has become like one of us, knowing good and evil; and now, lest he put forth his hand and take also of the tree of life, and eat, and live for ever'—therefore the Lord God sent him forth from the garden of Eden . . ." (Gen. 3:22, 23). This statement implies that the

---

[1] Scriptural references are from the Revised Standard Version, © 1946, 1952, by Division of Christian Education of the National Council of Churches of Christ in the United States of America.

[2] Gustave Friedrich Oehler, *Theology of the Old Testament,* translated by George E. Day (New York and London: Funk and Wagnalls Co., Inc., 1889), p. 157.

possibility of reaching immortality was closely related to the life in Paradise and as long as man lived in unbroken or harmonious communion with God, his life would continue on this earth.

Since God created man in his image (Gen. 1:26, 27) it was the purpose of the Almighty that man should live and not die. When man succumbed to sin, or disobedience, the corruption of disharmony weakened the body and death ensued.

Paradise's immortal strength may be evidenced in the extremely long earthly lives of Adam, Methuselah, Jacob and others mentioned in the Bible. We must remember, too, that God's image in man cannot be destroyed by the physical death of the body in which it dwells. It was God's intention that man should be immortal. Although sin has weakened the physical body through which man expresses his life here on earth, by the grace of God man lives with or without his body.

Hebrew Conceptions of Death and Immortality

"When thou hidest thy face, they are dismayed; when thou takest away their breath, they die and return to their dust" (Ps. 104:29). The ancient Hebrews believed that death occurs when the divine spirit which keeps man alive is withdrawn from the body by God. The body then returns to the dust whence it came.

In contrast to ancient Egyptian theology, Hebrew thought did not make life after death contingent upon the preservation of the body. But, Hebrew thought did make the spirit of man less conscious without the body. There may have been some thought that the soul still subsists in the body for a short while, at least, after death. This was expressed in Job 14:22, "He feels only the pain of his own body, and he mourns only for himself." Job was speaking of death when he made that statement.

However, Job also said in 34:14, 15, "If he should take back his spirit to himself, and gather to himself his breath, all flesh would perish together, and man would return to dust."

Because man is a vital being when spirit and body are together, it was believed that the spirit, when fully withdrawn from the body, continued to exist as a weak shadow wandering in the kingdom of the dead.[3]

The place where the souls migrated was called *Sheol*. It is of interest that language students trace the stem of the original Hebrew to a word that means "ravine, an abyss or to be hollow." From this stem in German we have *Hoehle* which means "cavern" and *Hoelle* which means "hell."

Sheol was thought to be in the depths of the earth, even deeper than the waters of the sea. It was a place of darkness (Job 10:22) where the dead were assembled in tribes. A number of passages in the Old Testament refer to death as being gathered to his father or his people. The term "pit" is also used to designate the abode of the dead.

That the spirit would retain its identity in Sheol is clearly indicated. Jacob, mourning the loss of Joseph whom he thought was destroyed by a wild beast, refused to be comforted and lamented, "No, I shall go down to Sheol to my son, mourning" (Gen. 37:35).

Like in sleep, the spirits of the departed were thought to rest in quietness in a land of forgetfulness (Ps. 88:12, Ps. 94:17, Ps. 115:17). However, consciousness was not destroyed and was thought to be capable of being aroused. There is only one example in the Old Testament of a spirit being called from the dead and that is of Samuel (I Sam. 28:8–19).

However, it was believed that the dead spirits could be awakened and necromancy was strongly forbidden. God charged the Hebrew people as they were about to enter the land of Canaan, "There shall not be found among you any one . . . who practices divination, a soothsayer, or an augur, or a sorcerer, or a charmer, or a medium, or a wizard, or a necromancer. For whoever does these things is an abomination to the Lord" (Deut. 18:10, 11, 12).

There seems to have been no difference in the lot of those who were in the realm of the dead (Job 3:17–19), only division

---

[3] *Ibid.*, pp. 169–170.

into tribes and races, not just and unjust.[4] It was an existence of neither blessedness nor unhappiness. Death was regarded as the curse of God that hangs over man as a punishment for his sin. There are only two individuals in the Old Testament who were spared death: Enoch (Gen. 5:24) and Elijah (II Kings 2:1–12). At the same time the relation of the righteous to God was not cancelled in death, for the blood of the murdered Abel cried to God (Gen. 4:10). Long after the patriarchs had died, God referred to Himself as the God of Abraham, Isaac and Jacob. Ecclesiastes 12:7 speaks of the spirit that returns to God who gave it.

Throughout the Old Testament there is evidence of beliefs in the immortality of the spirit of man. God reaches down to the realm of the dead and is omnipresent there. The soul's longing for the presence of God would be satisfied there in peace and quietness forever.

Early Christian Beliefs About Death and Immortality

Jesus, the Son of God, came and dwelt among men to reveal the will of God for man's temporal and eternal welfare. Jesus taught that the soul of man is eternal (Matt. 10:28, Matt. 16:26, Matt. 19:16, Matt. 25:46, Mark 10:30, John 6:39, John 10:28, John 11:25, 26, John 14:19).

Jesus also spoke in parables about the Kingdom of Heaven where the faithful would abide in eternal bliss in the presence of a loving God. In John 10, He stated specifically that He would give His life as an atonement for the sins of man. In His discourse with Nicodemus He made it explicit that "For God so loved the world that he gave his only Son, that whoever believes in him should not perish but have eternal life" (John 3:16).

On the cross He said to the repentant criminal, "Truly, I say to you, today you will be with me in Paradise" (Luke 23:43). This assurance indicates that the transition of the soul from the body to Paradise would be instantaneous.

However, He also spoke of His return in glory to judge all

---

[4] *Ibid.*, p. 173.

the nations (Matt. 25:31–46). At that time the righteous would inherit the kingdom prepared for them from the foundation of the world. The unrighteous would be assigned to eternal punishment.

Heaven became for the ancient Christians the chief goal of attainment and the life in this world was regarded as a preparation for it. Death became for them a release, to be anticipated rather than feared.

"For to me to live is Christ, and to die is gain. . . . My desire is to depart and be with Christ, for that is far better" (Phil. 1:21, 23). These words of the Apostle Paul expressed the certainty of the believers in immortality in the presence of the Lord. There was nothing that they so much desired as to dwell in Heaven and death was regarded as the gateway to eternal bliss.

Many believed in the resurrection of a transformed body. Whereas the ancient Egyptians placed the soul into a resuscitated body and the ancient Hebrews believed that the soul would be less conscious in Sheol without the body, many Christians believed that Christ would soon return in all His glory and the dead would be called forth from the grave in a body resembling the resurrected body of Jesus.

An ancient treatise on Hades, attributed by some scholars to Josephus and regarded as spurious by others, states clearly the current belief. "Although it (the body) be dissolved for a time on account of the original transgression, it exists still, and is cast into the earth as into a furnace, in order to be formed again, not in order to rise again such as it was before, but in a state of purity, and so as never to be destroyed any more."[5]

Other ancient believers were concerned that only the soul survive in heaven with the Lord. Death was the blessed process that released the spirit from the burden of the flesh. They regarded death as "the day of victory."[6] Christian martyrs anticipated death in order to be with Jesus. They visioned the Lord's

---

[5] *The Works of Josephus,* trans. by William Whiston, A.M. (Hartford, Conn.: S. S. Scranton Co., 1916), p. 928.

[6] Herbert B. Workman, M.A., *Persecution in the Early Church* (Cincinnati: Jennings and Graham, 1906), pp. 317, 318.

trumpeting angels welcoming each sufferer into the heavenly realm.

John T. McNeill states that many Christians were sent to the unspeakable cruelty of the mines by their persecutors. Cyprian wrote a moving letter full of heartfelt admiration for their martyrdom. The beatings, chains, filth, hunger and labor they endured are severely contrasted with the heavenly rewards awaiting them. The body is captive, but the heart reigns with Christ.[7]

Modern Conceptions of Death and Immortality

Today, there is no unanimity of concepts regarding death and immortality among believers, Christians or Jews. Many of the conclusions of the ancients influence our thinking. The idea that the soul leaves the body in death, as well as its immortality, seems to be unanimous. The concept of a heaven or a condition akin to it for the righteous does prevail in Christian and Jewish beliefs. However, there are many conceptions of the heavenly realm and God may will it to be so. If the soul is in a state of blessedness for those who are worthy of this condition, heaven, of necessity, would need to be in various states of spiritual being to satisfy many different personal requirements for perfect bliss.

Concepts of Hell

The concepts of hell vary also. Some regard it as a place of eternal torment for the wicked. Others believe that punishment serves no purpose if it is not disciplinary, and cannot accept the idea that a good God would eternally torment a soul unless the soul could benefit by it. Others contend that the very wicked deserve to suffer eternally and that transition of the soul to hell occurs immediately at the time of death.

Roman Catholic beliefs. Roman Catholic belief consigns to hell the very wicked and to purgatory the souls that depart in a state of grace but are guilty of excusable or not seriously wrong

----

[7] John T. McNeill, *A History of the Cure of Souls* (New York: Harper and Row, Publishers, 1951), p. 101.

sins. These souls are detained before entering heaven and are helped by the prayers of the faithful and they, in turn, may pray to God in behalf of those who thus remember them. They shall enter heaven either on the day of final judgment or when they have satisfied God's justice for their sins.

Those who die in grace, having received the sacraments and cooperated in the reception of them, go directly to heaven into the presence of the Lord.

No one can determine the precise moment when the soul takes its flight from the body. For that reason, the sacraments of Extreme Unction and Baptism can be administered as long as there is any of the original warmth of life in the body.

Jewish beliefs. The Jewish faith also attributes immortality to the soul. "Death is not the end; the earthly body vanishes, the immortal spirit lives with God. In our hearts, also, our loved ones never die. Their love and memory abide as a lasting inspiration, moving us to noble deeds and blessing us evermore."[8]

The soul is believed to enter the realm of eternal peace at once. "The departed whom we now remember have entered into the peace of life eternal. They still live on earth through acts of goodness they performed and in the hearts of those who cherish their memory."[9]

In the Prayer on the Anniversary of Death, the loved one is remembered: "Help me to feel that my dear _____ is in thy peaceful keeping. My dear _____ is gone; but all the goodness, the sweetness and nobility of that life I will remember. As this light burns pure and clear, so may the blessed memory of the goodness, the nobility of character of my dear _____ illumine my soul."[10]

Protestant beliefs. The ancient Egyptian belief in the resurrection or resuscitation of the body is held by some people today. The elaborate preparation of the body for burial and pre-

---

[8] *The Union Prayerbook for Jewish Worship* (Cincinnati: The Central Conference of American Rabbis, 1947), p. 275.

[9] *Ibid.*, p. 276.

[10] *Ibid.*, p. 384.

cautions taken to preserve it against disintegration may be interpreted by some as efforts to keep it as long as possible for the habitation of the soul on the day of resurrection.

That the body will be resurrected is believed by many Christians, and within the concepts of the early church, that it will be a purified body without the corruption of sin (I Cor. 15:35–50), resembling the resurrected body of Jesus.

Instant Sanctification

Most Protestants believe in the instant sanctification of the saved. The "saved" are those who accept Jesus as their personal Saviour at some time during life and thereafter live in accordance with God's will as close as possible. Even a deathbed confession of faith in Him is acceptable. While most Protestants believe that a person should be baptized (either immersed or sprinkled) as a sign of repentance and faith, many believe that a deathbed confession will be sufficiently acceptable to God to assure life with Him in heaven. Generally, Protestants will not baptize an unconscious person.

Instant sanctification assumes that the soul immediately goes to heaven. "Now he is at rest," or "Now, the suffering is over and he is with the Lord," are typical expressions of this belief. When a person is known to be an unbeliever and/or very wicked, it is assumed that the soul immediately migrates to hell. "Now he'll get what he deserves," is the popular expression of this conviction.

Universal Salvation

Other believers contend that eventually everyone will be saved. This conception is based on Romans 5:18, "Then as one man's trespass led to condemnation for all men, so one man's act of righteousness leads to acquittal and life for all men." The words of Jesus in John 12:32 may be construed to mean that eventually all shall be saved in heaven. According to this view God loves everyone and is able to save all. That this may be accomplished for the wicked, it is held that following death these souls will be given an opportunity to repent and believe or be punished until they do.

Destruction of the Wicked

Another view is that the wicked will be destroyed. This concept is also expressed in the New Testament, "They shall suffer the punishment of eternal destruction and exclusion from the presence of the Lord and from the glory of his might" (II Thess. 1:9). Their destruction is a punishment that prevents them from the joy and bliss experienced in the presence of the Lord.

Time of Death

There is also a difference of opinion relative to the time of death. Most Protestant and Jewish people accept the medical viewpoint that when a person stops breathing and the heart ceases its function the body is dead. Death means, for the believer, that the soul takes its flight from the mortal remains. So vivid is this belief even today that often, at the moment of death, a witness will open the window in the sickroom to facilitate the soul's flight to heaven. In some homes, all mirrors, especially those in the patient's room, will be covered with cloth or turned to the wall so the soul won't be confused in its journey to heaven.

As was mentioned previously, Roman Catholic doctrine does not state the exact time when the soul leaves the body.

In Conclusion

In conclusion, it may be said that Christian and Jewish people believe that man's soul is immortal but the conceptions of life after death vary considerably.

Underlying all Christian philosophy of death and immortality is the spiritual law of the harvest stated by the Apostle Paul in Galatians 6:7, "Do not be deceived; God is not mocked, for whatever a man sows, that he will also reap."

In ministering to the dying, the clergyman may bear in mind

that his parishioner is aware of this spiritual law. The patient
wants to be adequately prepared spiritually for death and what
it will mean for him in the eternal life. Members of the patient's
family, who are believers, will also be concerned about the spiritual state of the loved one.

There are various conceptions of heaven. Yet, in all the
variety there is still a common belief that a state of blessedness
will be the portion of the faithful. Whatever may be the factors
necessary for each individual will be provided there.

Another belief that is held by almost all Christians is that
faith in Jesus Christ as a personal Saviour is essential to a life in
Heaven. Christ has atoned for man's sins through His life and
His suffering and death upon the cross. Through His resurrec-
tion and ascension He made it possible for those who believe in
Him to dwell with Him in glory. Those who will attain eter-
nal bliss are those who accept Him through faith as a personal
Saviour.

Many Christians believe that good works have merit in at-
taining eternal bliss. This belief is based upon Jesus' description
of the last judgment in Matthew 25:31–46. When an individual
lives a life of purely selfish interests and shares little of his time,
talents and possessions with others, he cannot expect much consideration in the next life.

Unbelievers and wicked people will not inherit the Kingdom of Heaven. Most Christians do not sit in judgment over
others but leave it to the all-wise, omnipotent God to judge each
one according to his merits.

Most Christians believe that there is a hell; however, there
are many opinions of this place for the souls of the wicked. Some
believe in a literal hell of fire and brimstone where the wicked
will be tormented forever. A woman recently told me that her
"preacher" said that if a wicked person's leg or arm were paralyzed
or removed in this world, when the crippled one goes to hell the
appendage will be restored so it can feel pain also.

Others believe that hell serves no purpose, if it is not disciplinary. The wicked must reside there until they have "paid"

for their sins and accepted the Lord. How long this will take will depend upon the individual under God's judgment.

It is believed that God will deal with each one upon his merits and each will receive what he deserves, for in eternity the scales of justice are balanced, but with mercy and love.

These are some of the more prevalent conceptions of death and immortality with which the pastor will be confronted in his ministry to the dying. With very few exceptions, all of his people believe in some form of eternal life and look to him for guidance in preparing for it.

CHAPTER TWO

GETTING To The PATIENT
WHO IS DYING

Maintaining a pastoral relationship with a parishioner who is terminally sick may pose a problem for the clergyman, both physically and spiritually. When the patient is at home, the problem of getting physically near enough to converse comfortably and intimately probably will not be as complicated as in a hospital situation.

In the Home

Loved ones will want to be near the dying one constantly. This is understandable and should not be discouraged. They want to express their love and make the dear one's remaining days as comfortable as possible.

The pastor's visit is almost always appreciated. The patient may want to feel the touch of the pastor's hand on his own, particularly when the minister prays. The touch of the hand may be a means of spiritual communication. It has been used in the church since the days of the apostles to signify the transmission of the Holy Spirit and as an expression of sympathy, understanding, love and oneness in faith.

The presence of the pastor is also spiritually comforting. When the patient is in the home, the pastor may sit or stand near the bed where the patient can see him. If the minister and patient wish to speak in confidence, the pastor may ask the family for privacy.

When the patient desires Baptism, Holy Communion or Extreme Unction, family members may participate in the sacrament. Unless the situation is urgent, an appropriate time should be set when spouse or next of kin and children can be present. However, the sacrament must not be withheld for the family's convenience.

In one instance when a very sick woman expressed the desire to be baptized, her sister-in-law urged that the rite be administered when the patient's husband came home from work that evening. When the pastor returned, the patient was unconscious. In this instance, since she had expressed the desire, the pastor administered the sacrament (hoping that she could hear and feel what was being said and done) and prayed that the act would be acceptable to God.

In a Hospital

With the hospitalized patient the situation might be quite different as death approaches. The physician may order the patient to be placed under an oxygen tent. With an intravenous stand and bottle on one side of the bed and a drainage bottle on the other, it may be physically difficult for the minister to maintain an intimate pastoral relationship. As long as there is consciousness, the patient may want to clasp the pastor's hand in prayer. The minister may carefully reach under the cover of the tent and take the patient's hand in his.

In his hospital visits, the minister should proffer his card and introduce himself to the nurses. They need to know the patient's pastor as well as his doctor. He must not take for granted that he is known, unless he is readily recognized by his garb.

When Holy Communion is to be administered, he should inform the head nurse, who will see to it that the curtains are drawn around the bed to prevent any distractions. She may also inform the physician that this preparation for death has been done.

Roman Catholic

For the Roman Catholic patient, the same procedure is followed for Confession, Holy Communion and Extreme Unction. The priest prefers to be alone with the patient for Confession. However, when administering Holy Communion or Extreme

Unction, family members are encouraged to witness these min-
istries for the comfort they derive from knowing that their loved
one is spiritually prepared.

The "No Visitors" Sign

The "No Visitors" sign on the sickroom door may cause the
clergyman to wonder if this refers to him, too. It may be said that
the minister is one of the therapeutic team. The sign does not apply to hospital personnel, and it certainly should not exclude the
pastor whose ministry to a dying person is of utmost importance.
But it does mean that the pastor should always check with the
head nurse and inquire about the sign's meaning. If the family
wishes to exclude the pastor, he may learn from her why this was
done or he may consult the family about it. However, a minister
is rarely excluded and the sign is to discourage unwanted visitors,
too many friends or curious people who might disturb the patient.

If the nurse is reluctant to admit him, the minister may consult the physician to learn the significance of her attitude. In
some instances, the patient's faith is different from that of the
family who may want him "converted" before death. In such a
delicate situation he should first consult the physician and then
speak with the family to explain that if the patient wants his
ministry, he must not be denied it. I recall a widower and his
sister (his next of kin) who sat in his hospital room most of the
time. When his pastor called, she would not permit him to enter.
Once, during her absence, he called upon the patient, who responded, "Reverend, I am so glad you came."

"I have been here a number of times," the minister said,
"but I was prevented from seeing you."

"She is my sister," he said, "and she takes charge. She has
another minister calling on me. I told her I do not want to see
him, but it does no good. I wish she wouldn't do that and when
you come, come right in whether she likes it or not."

So, the pastor administered to his parishioner until he passed
away, but the sister called upon *her* minister for funeral services.

This man's pastor, in speaking about it later, said, "It was
embarrassing to me because the obituary stated that he was a

member of my church. But, I know that a funeral service is for the living, and his sister would not have appreciated anything that I said or did."

"Did the other minister call you or invite you to participate in the service?" I asked.

"No, he did not," was his only comment.

Unfortunately, such ministerial discourtesies do occur at times.

The sister's pastor was also placed in a delicate position when he was asked to call upon this patient. Ethically, instead of acceding to the sister's wishes, he should have called the patient's pastor, explained his predicament and refused to call any more. A minister has no more right to call upon another pastor's parishioner than a doctor has to call upon another doctor's patient. He also transgressed ethical standards when he accepted the call to conduct the funeral service and did not invite the man's pastor to participate. The patient's pastor might have contacted the other minister and kindly explained that his calls were disturbing the dying man. Everyone deserves to die with the peace of soul made possible by his religious beliefs. Only the parishioner's pastor, whom he knows and loves, can accord that privilege.

When a dying parishioner's family wants to exclude the patient's pastor from the sickroom, religious bigotry almost always has something to do with it. But, the pastor, by listening to the conscious patient, can be reassured if his ministry is comforting.

The "No Visitors" sign does not apply to a clergyman unless the patient prefers the ministry of another. Medically, when a doctor feels his patient's dissatisfaction, he may suggest that another physician be consulted. The same is true if a terminally sick parishioner desires another clergyman to visit him. The pastor should honor the request.

When the Patient Is Unconscious

When a patient is unconscious, spiritual communication is difficult. But the pastor must not conclude that his ministry does not penetrate the haze of unconsciousness. The patient's inability to respond does not mean that he is not conscious of what is being said and done.

A minister who experienced a severe heart attack was placed under an oxygen tent and sedated. Two women from his parish stood outside the door discussing his condition. He heard them say that he would not recover. In his unconscious condition he could not respond. When the hospital chaplain called some days later, the patient told him how the conversation had depressed him.

In some instances, when a member of the family places a finger in the hand of the unconscious person and asks the patient to squeeze it, there will be a response that clearly indicates that the patient can hear.

When all symptoms indicate that the patient is definitely unconscious, there is still the possibility of auditory perception. The pastor may continue his ministry on the assumption that the parishioner can hear his voice.

Some appropriate Scripture quotations may be spoken from the following selections: Psalm 23, John 10:1–18, Romans 8:31–39.

When offering prayer, if the pastor usually touches the patient's hand, he may follow the same practice with the unconscious person, for it offers reassurance and expresses love as well as a oneness in the faith. At the same time it is comforting to members of the family to know that their loved one is spiritually prepared either for life or for death.

CHAPTER THREE

SHOULD The PATIENT BE TOLD?

When a physician thinks that his patient is terminally sick, he may or may not share his opinion with the patient. Almost invariably, however, the next of kin will say, "I want to know the truth, doctor. Do you think he (or she) will recover?"

Most doctors are very kind and hesitate to state that they have no hope for recovery. "He is very sick," the doctor may reply, "and the outlook is not good." When a person dies suddenly, the physician may prefer that the family clergyman be present when he informs the next of kin.

If a pastor consults his parishioner's doctor, he probably will share the prognosis. If the doctor hesitates to confide in him, the pastor may explain that such information will be helpful in ministering to the patient and his family and will be regarded as confidential.

Loved ones often want to shield the patient by withholding information about his condition. "The doctor tells us there's no hope, but please don't let him know, Reverend," is a plea often heard by any clergyman. He may reassure the family that he will not tell the patient unless he insists on knowing. Then the minister explains that he does not want to endanger the relationship by being dishonest.

There are no statistics available either to prove or deny my personal observation that most terminally sick people do sooner or later realize the seriousness of their physical condition. When a patient for whom there is no hope for recovery says, "I don't think I'll recover," or "Do you think I'll ever get over this?," there is a realization that the sickness will be terminal.

When the Patient Wants To Know

Many sincere believers pray that God will protect them from sudden death. Because they are devout they are conscious of their unworthiness and want to spend their last moments on earth in repentance and prayer. Most people are not prepared for death and there are certain things they want to do or undo before the last moments of earthly life.

It is easy to comment that one should live each moment of life as if it were the last one, but few people do. Many sincere believers feel that they are not spiritually ready to die. Pastoral prayers in older manuals often plead with God to protect all believers from a bad, sudden death that would take them unprepared for it.[1] "If I were going to die, I would want to know it so I could be better prepared for it," is a statement pastors often hear.

When a terminally sick parishioner says plainly to his pastor in confidence, "I'm sure I'll never recover from this," it is not helpful for the minister to reply, "You must not talk like that. Get those ideas out of your head."

The patient's statement clearly indicates that he wants to talk with his pastor about the seriousness of his condition. The pastor may be permissive and encourage him to speak his thoughts about it. There may be spiritual problems that the patient wants to discuss. Instead of reassuring him that he will recover or telling him that he should not think about death, the minister may acknowledge that no one can predict when a person will die, but we do want to be spiritually prepared for either life or death. This provides the sick person with an opportunity to confide any concerns or hopes that he may have: he should always be made to feel free to talk openly with his pastor.

When the minister called on one elderly widow, her brother always discouraged talk about death. "I know the Lord will call me soon," she said.

---

[1] *Evangelische Agende, Evangelischen Synode des Westens* (St. Louis: Aug. Wiebusch and Son, 1875). Translated from p. 7.

Brother: "She mustn't talk that way. I tell her to quit talking about it."

She: "I want to say, Reverend, I have only my brother, and the church means so much to me I . . ."

Brother: "There's plenty of time to talk about that."

Pastor: "Would you like to talk with me alone?"

Brother: "She can say anything she wants to, I don't care."

She: "Could we talk alone?"

Pastor (to brother): "If you don't mind, please let us talk a few moments in privacy." (The brother reluctantly left the room.)

She: "When I die I want you to see to it that this house goes to the church. I have never done much for the Lord . . . my brother can have the rest."

Pastor: "Have you made a will?"

She: "No. My brother does not want me to . . . so I'm telling you."

Pastor: "What you tell me will not mean a thing unless you have a will. If you want me to do it, I will call Mr. . . . and ask him to draw up a will for you."

A few days later she passed away, but evidently the brother had either refused to admit Mr. . . . or talked her out of making a will. He inherited all of her property but gave a set of dishes to the church.

Other terminally sick parishioners may want to discuss the possibility of knowing loved ones in the eternal life.

After an Accident or Serious Surgery

When a parishioner asks if he will recover after a serious accident or surgery, the pastor should not attempt to answer the question. Only the physician may know the patient's physical condition. The minister may reply that he does not know the patient's physical condition and will offer prayers for recovery as in the following case.

An adolescent boy's skull was opened in a car accident and portions of the brain were exposed. The neurosurgeon was preparing to take him to surgery. The boy's parents were frantic with anxiety. "Will he live? . . . Do you think he will live?" the mother implored.

The chaplain thought that the lad had small chance for recovery, but, aware of the surgeon's skill and the power of prayer he said, "Only God knows the answer to your question, but He does invite us to come to Him with our prayers. I suggest that we do that and resign ourselves to His will in this situation."

The boy did recover and is well and healthy today.

When the Patient Does Not Want To Know

Many people fear death. Almost anyone is apprehensive about a new, unknown experience. A patient may not want to be told that his illness is terminal.

Mr. A was middle-aged when his physician referred him to a medical clinic for tests. The diagnosis was Hodgkin's disease. One of the physicians thought that since the patient was well educated and had business responsibilities, he should be told that he may have only two more years to live. This would give him time to arrange his affairs.

Mr. A became very depressed and resorted to alcohol. Later he added sedatives to the alcohol. As a result, he spent most of the last year and a half of his life under constant sedation and intoxication. Time and again he confided to his pastor that he wished he had not been told . . . that he could have gone on living his life with hope.

Mr. B, another patient, was diagnosed as terminally sick with cancer, but was not told. Mr. B was married and had a grown son and daughter. His sister was a very religious woman and approached their mutual pastor about her brother's spiritual condition.

"Reverend," she said, "I think you should tell my brother that he is not going to recover."

"Why do you think that I should tell him?" the pastor asked.

"Because he doesn't know the Lord," she replied.

"Would you tell me what gives you that impression?" he asked.

"I just know that he doesn't know the Lord. He smokes and at times he takes a drink," she replied.

"Have you ever talked with him about these things?" the minister inquired.

"Yes, I have," she replied. "But I've gotten nowhere. He always tells me that he is all right and to mind my own business."

"As you know," the pastor remarked, "he does attend church and partakes of Holy Communion. Don't you think that this is an indication that he loves the Lord? Do you think he would do these things if he did not know the Lord?"

"It takes more than church membership to save a soul," she argued.

"Has your brother ever indicated to you that he would want to be told about his condition? Has he asked?" the minister inquired.

"No . . . he hasn't," she replied.

"Do his wife and family agree with you that he should be told?" he asked.

"She hasn't said anything to me about it," she said.

"Don't you think that in time he will realize his condition and at present, if he suspects it, he just doesn't want anyone to come straight out and tell him?" he asked.

"That may be the case," she acceded.

"Under the circumstances it would not be wise for me to tell him that he will not recover. It would spoil our fine relationship and furthermore, I'm not so certain that he won't. God has something to say about these matters, also. If your brother has any spiritual problems I'm sure he'll confide in me. At present his religious beliefs seem to be meeting his spiritual needs."

A believer's wishes in this matter should be respected. Generally, the patient suspects death anyway, but doesn't want anyone to be frank with him. Usually, there are emotional reasons for this attitude which should be respected. However, he may want to confide to the pastor the reasons for the attitude.

When the Family Wants the Patient To Know

In the case of Mr. B, neither his wife nor his children asked the minister to tell him and apparently they were not worried about his spiritual condition. In another situation, that of Mr. C, his wife was worried about his soul and wanted the pastor to tell him.

Mr. C was in his late 60's and never attended church, but he had been baptized as an infant. He was a professional gambler who had made a precarious living for his wife and two children. Mrs. C belonged to the church and attended it regularly. When Mr. C suffered a stroke, she asked her pastor to visit him. The doctor warned that her husband might have another stroke at any time, and that it could be fatal.

The minister called on Mr. C, whose right side was paralyzed, and tried to establish rapport with him. At first Mr. C was reticent about conversing with the pastor. Undoubtedly he was uncomfortable in the minister's presence and thought that the pastor would reproach him for his spiritual negligence. Instead, the minister kindly accepted him as he was and encouraged him to talk about his life. Mr. C expressed feelings of guilt when he rationalized that he made a living, on a small scale, doing what stock brokers on Wall Street do in a bigger way.

The minister neither argued nor agreed with this view. Instead, he led him into thoughts about his spiritual life, faith in God and prayer. After the second call, Mrs. C accompanied the minister to his car and expressed concern because he had not told Mr. C how serious his physical condition was. "I think you should tell him that the doctor thinks he may have another stroke at any moment."

The minister explained that he did not want to frighten Mr. C, for that might cause another stroke and then she and the doctor would blame him for it. It was enough to hope that God would grant Mr. C enough time to grow in repentance and faith.

During the third call, the patient accepted the pastor's offer to pray for him. However, Mr. C interrupted him in the prayer and asked him to explain what he meant by being "grateful to God for the saving grace of Jesus."

Mrs. C scolded her husband for interrupting the prayer, but the minister was glad for the opportunity to talk about achieving our Lord's grace through faith and repentance. A fine pastoral relationship developed thereafter. Mr. C became aware of the fact that he might have another stroke. It came naturally in the conversations and there was no necessity of making it a point to tell him. In the ensuing visits the pastor read to him selected Scripture passages which they discussed. Mr. C expressed great interest and welcomed the pastor's calls. A few months later the doctor's prediction came true when Mr. C was found dead one morning.

Loved ones may deeply desire the comforting assurance that a dying one has made some spiritual preparation for the life to come. However, it should not be regarded as solely the minister's responsibility to tell the patient. If he is convinced that the patient will benefit by telling him, he may discuss the serious nature of the sickness with the patient.

When the nearest of kin wants the patient to be told of his condition, the pastor should always try to ascertain the reasons for the attitude. In some cases, the next of kin wants the patient to know for reasons other than his spiritual welfare, such as the absence of a will. The pastor may counsel with the sick person regarding a will. Everyone should make provisions for the distribution of personal property after death. Usually such foresight makes for better family relationships. In discussing a will, the pastor may suggest that the patient remember his favorite charities, too.

When the Physician Does Not Want the Patient To Know

Usually the physician is well aware of his patient's emotional condition. In the case of a prolonged sickness, he may prefer that the patient not know, at least for awhile.

Perhaps the doctor is hoping his patient may be an exception to the rule and will recover. He doesn't want emotional disturbances to retard the healing process.

However, many physicians want their patients to be prepared for death when it happens. When the doctor does not want the patient to know, he usually has good reason. A clergyman respects the doctor's wishes in this matter, unless the pastor is concerned about the patient's spiritual state. In that event, he consults the physician and ascertains the reason for his attitude and explains his own concern. A pastor should not oppose the physician unless the patient shows no signs of repentance and faith.

The eternal welfare of the patient's soul is the pastor's responsibility. With humility and kindness he may counsel the patient into an understanding of the importance of the repentance and faith as essential to either life or death.

The Roman Catholic View

The Roman Catholic view is that the patient has an undeniable right to know the seriousness of his condition so that he can prepare properly for death.[2] Otherwise, he might refuse the sacraments and do himself a grave injustice.

If the patient asks the priest if he is going to die, the priest may assure him that God must decide this. However, if the patient refuses the sacraments, the priest, as a last resort, ought to explain to the doctor that the patient is in need of spiritual aid and suggest that the physician tell him that he is *in extremis*.[3] If the physician declines, the priest may tell him or have the family take care of it.

Under ordinary circumstances, those who are in danger of death should be advised of their condition so they will welcome the sacrament of Extreme Unction. It cannot harm them, and it often helps them.[4]

---

[2] Patrick O'Brian, C. M., *A Handbook for Hospital Chaplains* (St. Louis and London: B. Herder Book Co., 1959), p. 244.

[3] *Ibid.*, p. 245.

[4] John A. O'Brien, Ph.D., *The Catholic Faith, An Official Edition of the Revised Baltimore Catechism No. 3.* (Notre Dame, Ind.: Ave Maria Press, 1954), p. 246.

The Jewish View

The concepts of heaven and hell are foreign to Judaism. Judaism teaches that after death the soul returns to God's intimate presence to be judged along with all other souls. They do not speculate or try to define the nature of eternal life, leaving that entirely as God's responsibility. They believe that all Israel has a share in the world to come but do not try to describe that share.

Conservative rabbis rely upon the physician's advice regarding whether a dying patient should be told about his condition. If the physician thinks that this information will help the patient to "set his household in order," or change his attitude toward others and thereby benefit himself or his family, he should be told.

When the rabbi believes the patient is dying he may recite the Twenty-third Psalm. This is followed with "Hear, O Israel, the Lord is our God, the Lord is One," said once.

"Blessed be the Name of His Glorious Kingdom forever and forever," may be repeated three times.

While the patient is expiring, the rabbi may recite seven times, "The Eternal, He is God."

After the patient has expired, the rabbi speaks, "The Lord hath given, and the Lord hath taken away, blessed be the name of the Lord forever."

As a final word of adoration, the rabbi may say, "Blessed art Thou, O Lord our God, King of the Universe who is the Righteous Judge. Amen." If others are present they may join their voices with that of the rabbi in the "Amen."[5]

The Protestant View

Most Protestant clergy share the Roman Catholic belief that a person should be spiritually prepared for death by being at peace with God and man.

---

[5] Personally from Rabbi Martin Douglas of Temple Adath Israel in Evansville, Indiana. (Conservative.)

In some Protestant churches Holy Communion is observed as a last rite; in others, anointing is practiced. In nearly all churches, repentance, the acceptance of Jesus as a personal Saviour, and fellowship with the believers are considered as essential elements in the spiritual preparation for the eternal life.

When the pastor believes the dying person to be in communion with God and at peace with his fellowmen, it is not necessary for the pastor to tell the patient that death is approaching. However, if the parishioner harbors resentments, is without repentance and gives little evidence of faith, it may be necessary for the pastor to remind the dying person of the serious nature of the sickness.

Most Protestants regard baptism as an evidence of repentance and faith and believe that a dying person should be baptized, if the patient has not previously received this sacrament. Most Protestant clergy recognize the baptism of any denomination as valid, including that of the Roman Catholic church.

Those who accept only immersion may regard the sincere faith and good intentions of the dying person as a substitute for baptism and usually do not insist that a dying person be immersed.

When the doctor or members of the family do not want the terminally sick person to be told and the Protestant minister feels strongly that he should be informed for the benefit of his soul, the clergyman may express the reasons for his concern. He must, in fairness, weigh the merits of the objections. He may have underestimated the spirituality of the patient.

If, after due consideration and consultation, he concludes that either or both the physician and family members are not interested in the eternal welfare of the dying person, he may need to do as the Roman Catholic priest is instructed: to minister to the spiritual needs of the dying person, for every person has the right to die in peace with God and man. At the same time, he may try to meet the spiritual needs of the loved ones who are unconcerned about the eternal life.

Since the pastor will minister mostly to people of his parish, instances of the latter nature will be rare; but he will be confronted with them occasionally and should be prepared for such situations.

CHAPTER FOUR

SPECIFIC SITUATIONS

A clergyman's ministry to the dying will vary according to the situation, the patient's beliefs, the attitudes of the family, religious customs and the pastor's own convictions. There is no defined formula or procedure that every Protestant pastor can apply to every situation.

Ministering to the dying is the most challenging of all pastoral functions, for the clergyman will need to be spiritually and emotionally sensitive to the needs of the individual and the members of the loved one's family. To be helpful, he must communicate understanding, love and faith with a great deal of the guidance of the Holy Spirit.

However, there are some typical patterns of spiritual needs, adjustments and expressions in specific situations that the pastor may use as guides in his ministry to the dying.

Almost every "normal" person craves security and love, in this world and in the one to come. While we are here on earth we rely largely upon our possessions and our loved ones for these. At the same time, most believers are convinced that God takes care of His own. We believe that through faith in Him we have spiritual security. Our loved ones and our material possessions may help to confirm this belief.

We also know that the earth is an "Indian Giver" that takes back at death everything that it has bestowed, including loved ones and possessions. The dying one is usually aware of this, and what he believes will be extremely important to his feelings of security and to the pastor in his ministry to him.

If the patient believes that his loved ones will have a reasonable measure of security in this world, it will eliminate at least one worry. Belief that loved ones will be united in eternity helps the dying person ease the emotional strain that accompanies thoughts about parting. When the dying one has used a portion of the personal possessions "to lay up treasures in heaven," or to do "good works," this will give the dying one feelings of security and moderate any fears of God.

When the Pastor Needs to Consult Another Minister

In certain instances the pastor may need to consult with another one in meeting the spiritual needs of a dying person. Recently the wife of a man who was dying of cancer came to me in her anxiety. "A better husband and father never lived," she said with tears in her eyes. "But, he has never been baptized. Would you please baptize him before he dies?"

"I will," I said, "if he desires to express his repentance and faith with this sacrament."

"He does," she said. "You can talk with him."

"Do you have a pastor," I asked, "and have you consulted with him about this?"

"We are Baptists," she replied, "and our minister baptizes only by immersion."

"I will talk with your pastor, if you will give me his name," I said, "and thereafter either he or I will baptize him."

I called the pastor on the phone and his response in substance was, "I baptize only by immersion, so you go right ahead and do it."

This is mentioned here because the pastor must be guided by the parishioner's beliefs in helping the dying one find a measure of spiritual security. Ecclesiastical regulations and denominational restrictions should not be used to prevent a dying person from expressing his or her religious convictions. When the minister is restricted in a specific religious area he may call upon another clergyman to assist him, as one physician may call another in consultation. Here, the patient had to take the initiative. It would have made for a better future pastoral relationship with the wife of the dying man if the pastor had taken the initiative and called another minister to care for the patient's specific spiritual need.

Using the Patient's Spiritual Merits

The minister cannot prepare any person to die. He may use the rites of the Church for that purpose, but in the last analysis, what the dying one believes and the manner in which he has lived is the preparation for death, and only God can evaluate these merits. The clergyman fulfills his calling by assisting the person in using his spiritual resources to meet his needs for security in relation to his eternal welfare.

The Patient with Cancer

Cancer is one of the most dreaded of all diseases. Fortunately, the stigma that once accompanied cancer has now largely vanished from our thinking and the patient does not have to contend with feelings of shame in addition to the other emotional aspects that accompany the disease.

Hope. Most cancer patients harbor some hope for recovery. They know that in its advanced stages it is seldom cured, but almost everyone hopes to be an exception to the rule. Any temporary improvement in the physical condition will be accepted by the patient, and usually by loved ones also, as a token or sign that the patient is getting better. The pastor will notice, for example, when the patient has been able to sustain a little food, perhaps a few spoons of gelatin or sips of juice, the reaction will be, "I think I am some better today."

Thus, the truth dawns slowly upon the patient that the disease will be terminal. Whereas the patient might experience emotional shock if told at one time that the disease cannot be cured, temporary improvements that become less and less frequent give the dying one more time to adjust to the inevitable.

The type of treatment that is offered often causes the patient to be aware of the nature of the disease. In many instances the patient is aware of the situation but refrains from talking about it with loved ones.

Shielding loved ones. The pastor will listen carefully to
the patient when other members of the family are not present.
Mrs. D, 40, was released from the hospital to remain home as long
as possible. Her diagnosis was cancer in an advanced stage. Her
pastor called upon her often and suspected her condition; however, she never mentioned cancer until one afternoon when he
was alone with her.

"I know I have cancer, Reverend," she confided, "and I
doubt if I'll get well, but I hate to tell my husband because I
know he'll go all to pieces if I do."

"Do you think your husband suspects it anyway?" the pastor
asked.

"I don't think so. At first I thought that perhaps the doctor
would tell him. But he always talks about what we will do when
I get my health back again."

"Has the doctor told you that you will not get well again?"
the pastor asked cautiously.

"Not in so many words," she responded. "But I can tell by
little things he says and by the treatments I received this last time
in the hospital. He did surgery the first time but now he doesn't
suggest it any more."

"Have you asked the doctor?" he responded.

"Yes, I have," she said. "But his answer is evasive. He says,
'You make up your mind to get well and we'll talk about that
later.' "

"Do you think it would be helpful to you if you would share
your thoughts with your husband?" he asked.

"I wish I could," she said, "but I'm afraid for him. Would
you do me a favor?"

"I will be pleased to do so if I can," he responded carefully.

"Please talk with Gary [their 16-year-old son]. I don't know
what has come over him. He's changed so much. I can't get him
to attend church or youth meetings. That's not like Gary. I've
asked him to tell me what's wrong and all he says is, 'Nothing's
wrong, Mom, I just don't want to go.' We never had any trouble
with him like that before."

A few moments later Gary came home from school and ran up the stairs to his mother's room. He appeared to be a bit startled at first, although he must have seen the minister's car parked at the curb. He spoke a cold "Hello" and leaned over to kiss his mother.

"I just now asked our minister to talk with you, Gary," she said kindly. "I wish you would do that for me."

"Oh . . . all right," he said reluctantly.

Suddenly aware of the change in Gary's attitude, the pastor decided to talk with him at that time. "If you will excuse us," he said to Mrs. D, "we'll leave the room and talk."

Seated on a couch downstairs, the pastor started, "Gary, we've been friends for a number of years. I believe you know me well enough to trust me. Your mother is worried about the change in your attitude toward the church. Would you tell me what has happened? I'd like to help if you will let me."

Tears came to Gary's eyes as he responded, "I can't talk in here."

"Will it help if we go and sit in my car?" the minister asked kindly.

Seated in the car, Gary said, "I guess you know Mom is going to die. She doesn't know it but Dad does. He told me. I hate God. Why does He have to do this to Mom? Why? She's only 40 years old. Why does God make her die?"

"And I suppose you don't like me anymore because you think that I'm on God's side. Is that right, Gary?" the minister asked.

"I don't know," he hesitated, and then, "Oh, well, I might as well say it, you're right."

"I can understand why you blame God and me," the minister responded. "I suppose I'd feel the same way if this happened to me and I didn't understand. There are times for me, too, when I have to pray a lot, when I don't understand why things have to happen as they do."

"You mean that sometimes you get mad at God, too?" Gary asked.

"Perhaps that's about the way to say it," the minister explained. "But only when I don't understand. You see, Gary, we think we know a lot, and we do, but we don't know everything. When we don't understand, we are inclined to blame God."

"I'll go along with you on that, Reverend," Gary agreed. "It's just that I love Mom and I don't want her to be taken away. A lot of bad people live a long time. But Mom is good. She prays and she goes to church."

"I can fully understand how you feel about it because my mother has gone to heaven and I didn't want her taken away from me either. But I believe you are glad that your mother is such a fine Christian woman. Am I right?"

"Yes. Because she's so good, I think God should let her live longer," he argued.

"In relation to her sickness, Gary, why are you relieved because she is a Christian?" he asked kindly.

"I get it. And that's right. I know she'll go to heaven . . ."

"And God will take care of her?" the minister said.

"And God will take care of her," Gary repeated.

"Just two more things, Gary. I don't think that you and your father need hesitate in talking with your mother about her sickness. It would help all three of you to have an understanding among yourselves so you can express your thoughts to each other. The second thing is that I am not saying that your mother will or will not recover. Evidently the doctor has told your father that she will not and we must rely upon his opinion. Now, I'd like to go back and talk to your mother. She likes for me to read to her from the Scripture and pray with her. Would you like to come with me?"

"O.K.," Gary said.

When they were together in the room, the pastor assured Mrs. D that she need not hesitate to discuss her problem with Gary and her husband.

Later, in ministering to Mrs. D, he found her to be much more at ease in discussing the seriousness of her condition. She told him that she was no longer worried about her husband's and Gary's reaction to the situation.

The pastor talked with her husband and son often during the ensuing weeks. He assisted them in mutually supporting each other after they accepted the situation and could speak freely about it. When the dying patient feels that he or she cannot speak freely with loved ones, this secrecy becomes an additional burden.

Guilt or fear. A dying parishioner may want to tell his pastor about feelings of guilt or fear. The clergyman must be permissive and give the patient opportunities to freely express any concerns.

Lest he offer reassurance prematurely, it must be borne in mind that any digression or sin may loom very important when one is about to die. Cancer patients usually linger longer and thus have more time for reflection. There may be misgivings about neglecting loved ones, or the church or God. Although the pastor may feel that the digression is being exaggerated far beyond its importance, he must try to understand the patient's anxiety and assist the dying one through repentance to an acceptance of God's redeeming love in Jesus, the Saviour.

Reassuring a repentant believer. In his reassurance to a repentant believer the pastor may use the following:

> Just as I am, without one plea
> But that Thy blood was shed for me,
> And that Thou bidd'st me come to Thee,
> O Lamb of God, I come, I come!
> Just as I am! Thou wilt receive,
> Wilt welcome, pardon, cleanse, relieve;
> Because Thy promise I believe,
> O Lamb of God, I come, I come!
> *from a hymn by Charlotte Elliot*

Appropriate Scripture readings might be as follows:

> My son, do not regard lightly the discipline of the Lord, nor lose courage when you are punished by him. For the Lord disciplines him whom he loves, and chastises every son whom he receives.
> *Hebrews 12:5, 6*

For thus says the Lord: . . . I will visit you, and I will fulfill to you my promise and bring you back to this place. For I know the plans I have for you, says the Lord, plans for welfare and not for evil, to give you a future and a hope. Then you will call upon me and come and pray to me, and I will hear you. You will seek me and find me; when you seek me with all your heart, I will be found by you, says the Lord. . . .

Jeremiah 29:10–14

Seek the Lord while he may be found, call upon him while he is near; let the wicked forsake his way, and the unrighteous man his thoughts; let him return to the Lord, that he may have mercy on him, and to our God, for he will abundantly pardon.

Isaiah 55:6–7

Truly, truly, I say to you, he who hears my word and believes him who sent me, has eternal life; he does not come into judgment, but has passed from death to life.

John 5:24

A Prayer of Repentance for a Dying Person

Lord God, our heavenly Father,
With contrite hearts we turn to Thee.
We have often been unmindful of Thy love,
And sinned against Thee in thought, word and deed.
In deep humility we implore Thy forgiveness.
Help us to feel the healing forces
Of Thy forgiving love and saving grace;
Through the merits of our blessed Lord.
Grant unto us a sincere purpose
Henceforth so to live in accordance to Thy will,
That we may experience Thy Presence,
Day by day;
And growing in grace, receive us at last
In Thy glorious eternal Kingdom,
Through Jesus Christ, our Saviour.   Amen.

When one is afraid. It is natural for one to fear the unknown. The cancer patient may fear what the future may bring in suffering, medical costs and most of all, death itself. "The fear of the Lord is the beginning of knowledge" (Proverbs 1:7) is a wise statement. Only the proud would presume that they are sufficiently worthy to approach God through their own merits.

Fear may serve creative spiritual purposes in that it may direct the dying one humbly through repentance to an acceptance of God's grace. The pastor may be very helpful to the one who is afraid by assisting the parishioner into an experience of comfort in the presence of God.

A hymn, written long ago by Anna Waring, expresses the confidence that may grow out of fear:

> In heavenly love abiding,
> No change my heart shall fear;
> And safe in such confiding,
> For nothing changes here.
> The storm may roar without me,
> My heart may low be laid;
> But God is round about me,
> And can I be dismayed?

The Holy Scripture speaks to our fears:

> In peace I will both lie down and sleep;
> for thou alone, O Lord, makest me dwell in safety.
>
> *Psalm 4:8*

> The Lord is my light and my salvation;
> whom shall I fear?
> The Lord is the stronghold of my life;
> of whom shall I be afraid?
>
> *Psalm 27:1*

> When I am afraid,
> I put my trust in thee.
> In God, whose word I praise,
> in God I trust without a fear.
> What can flesh do to me?
>
> *Psalm 56:3–4*

If God is for us, who is against us? He who did not spare his own Son but gave him up for us all, will he not also give us all things with him? Who shall bring any charge against

God's elect? It is God who justifies; who is to condemn? Is it
Christ Jesus, who died, yes, who was raised from the dead,
who is at the right hand of God, who indeed intercedes for
us? Who shall separate us from the love of Christ? Shall tribulation, or distress, or persecution, or famine, or nakedness, or
peril, or sword? . . . No, in all these things we are more
than conquerors through him who loved us.

Romans 8:31–35, 37

A Prayer for One Who Is Afraid

Blessed God, our heavenly Father;
Thou hast been our guide and comfort
Along life's way until today;
Thou hast blessed us in so many ways
For which we are devoutly thankful.
Help us, O Lord, always to remember
That Thou hast invited us to come to Thee
For help in all our needs.
Now we call upon Thee.
Through Jesus, Thou hast redeemed us,
And spread the mantle of Thy love o'er us;
What time we are afraid, enfold us
With Thy Spirit in the comfort of Thy arms
Where we can find release from fear,
And the peace and confidence that we seek.
Remove from the mind and heart
Any undue worry or concern
As we rest our souls in Thee.   Amen.

When there is much suffering. When there is much
pain, the time seems longer than it really is. When a loved one
is spared a lengthened period of illness, relatives are usually
thankful, amidst the sorrow of parting, that the deceased was
saved from a longer time of suffering.

Modern medication, administered by a wise physician, can
alleviate much of the pain, but not all of it as long as the patient
is conscious. We do not know if an unconscious person experiences pain. Those who return to consciousness usually do not
remember if they suffered pain or not.

As long as the patient can converse with the pastor, the sedation helps to alleviate much of the pain that would otherwise torment the dying one. However, when the dosages must be increased, the patient may become irrational at times. But there are also lucid moments and the pastor will want to take these into consideration while ministering to the dying one.

When there is much suffering, even the most devout person may question God's love and experience periods of depression. When faith wavers, the pastor's presence, in itself, may have a stabilizing influence. The faithful usually do not want to lose their confidence in God and are seriously disturbed when that happens.

The clergyman must not become disconcerted when a faithful one questions God's love or expresses antagonism toward God. The pastor must guard against arguing, for God's love and integrity are not solely dependent upon the minister's arguments. To argue with a disturbed faithful one may engender antagonism toward the pastor which will add still another stress. The pastor's understanding and demeanor, under such conditions, communicates God's love and helps to confirm the patient's wavering faith.

The pastor will be helpful by being permissive so the patient will have an opportunity to give expression to any doubts or feelings of hostility toward God. Then, with understanding and patience he may help the parishioner confirm his or her faith through counseling rather than preaching.

The loved ones may also be much disturbed by the patient's attitude. The pastor may be helpful to them by explaining that prolonged suffering does affect one's thinking and the medication may also influence attitudes. He may invite them to be in the sickroom when he offers the patient reassurance from the Word of God and through prayer.

When a believer doubts God's love and care during prolonged or intense suffering, this reaction may be considered as "normal," for upon the cross our blessed Lord, in His anguish, also felt that God had forsaken Him. (Matt. 27:46; Mark 15:34) Through counseling and reassurance the pastor may assist the suffering one through disturbing doubts to an acceptance of his illness and reliance upon God's help to bear the burden with a benign spirit.

For one who is suffering the following reassurances may be helpful:

> In the hour of trial, Jesus plead for me;
> Lest by base denial I depart from Thee;
> When Thou see'st me waver, With a look recall,
> Nor for fear or favor Suffer me to fall.
>
> Should Thy mercy send me Sorrow, toil, or woe,
> Or should pain attend me On my path below,
> Grant that I may never Fail Thy hand to see;
> Grant that I may ever Cast my care on Thee.
>
> *from the hymn by J. Montgomery*

> Why are you cast down, O my soul,
> and why are you disquieted within me?
> Hope in God; for I shall again praise him,
> my help and my God.
>
> Deep calls to deep
> at the thunder of the cataracts;
> all thy waves and thy billows
> have gone over me.
> By day the Lord commands his steadfast love;
> and at night his song is with me,
> a prayer to the God of my life.
>
> *Psalm 42:5, 7–8*

> For affliction does not come from the dust,
> nor does trouble sprout from the ground;
> but man is born to trouble
> as the sparks fly upward.
> "As for me, I would seek God,
> and to God would I commit my cause;
> who does great things and unsearchable,
> marvelous things without number . . . "
>
> *Job 5:6–9*

It is for discipline that you have to endure. God is treating you as sons; for what son is there whom his father does not discipline? If you are left without discipline, in which all have participated, then you are illegitimate children and not sons.

Besides this, we have had earthly fathers to discipline us and we respected them. Shall we not much more be subject to the Father of spirits and live? For they disciplined us for a short time at their pleasure, but he disciplines us for our good, that we may share his holiness. For the moment all discipline seems painful rather then pleasant; later it yields the peaceful fruit of righteousness to those who have been trained by it.

Hebrews 12:7–11

A PRAYER FOR ONE WHO IS SUFFERING

Almighty God, our merciful Father,
Who dost tenderly care for us
Even in the midst of our afflictions,
Graciously help us to keep our trust in Thee.
Deliver us from our suffering
According to Thy holy will,
And grant that our afflictions may work for us
Eternal blessings and glory.
However dark the way may seem now
And heavy the burden of pain,
Grant that the night of our suffering
May dawn into a day of gladness.
Strengthen and comfort us with Thy Holy Spirit
That we may bear our burden
With patience and courage,
Looking to Thee for our salvation;
And in Thy good appointed time
Deliver us from all our afflictions
Through Jesus Christ, the heavenly Physician,
Our blessed Lord and Redeemer.   Amen

With a Heart Ailment

Feared equally with cancer are heart diseases. When the patient survives the initial attack, the recuperation period will vary according to the degree of heart damage and other health factors. Many people do recover from a heart attack. Seventy-five percent of those who survive an initial attack are still alive after five years, and as many as 70 percent stricken initially by arteriosclerotic heart disease are still alive ten years later.[1]

During the critical period (immediately following the initial attack), the minister may make many calls. It is not known if the patient will recover or experience another attack that may result in death. If the patient recovers there may be a long period of convalescence with intermittent days of depression.

The patient may be confined in an oxygen tent and/or be rather heavily sedated to induce relaxation and lessen any emotional or spiritual tensions. During this phase of the sickness the pastor's call will need to be brief, consisting mostly of reassurance unless the patient wishes to discuss a spiritual problem with him.

When the patient wants to talk about a tension or stress it is harmful therapy to refuse the desire, for to do so only tends to increase the tension. However, the pastor will refrain from broaching any subject that might cause the patient anxiety or tension.

A flagrant violation of this important principle of spiritual therapy of a critically sick heart patient was called to the hospital chaplain's attention by a nurse. She entered the room of an elderly woman heart patient who was under an oxygen tent. A man with an open Bible in his hand was arguing with her. Since the doctor had given specific orders to exclude visitors, she asked the man to identify himself. He told her that he was a prison and hospital chaplain called by God to convert criminals and the sick. She asked him to come with her and called the chaplain.

The chaplain met him and asked if he knew the patient or was a relative. He said No, but felt impelled to convert this woman because she was a Roman Catholic. She had proudly told him that one of her sons was a Roman Catholic priest.

The chaplain invited him to his office and tried to explain to him that people, whether they felt called by the Lord or not, could not be permitted to visit from room to room. The patients

---

[1] Averill and Kempf, *Psychology Applied to Nursing,* Fifth Edition, (Philadelphia: W. B. Saunders Company, 1956), p. 188.

would get no rest. Besides they had their own pastors or the hospital chaplain. (The chaplain tried to counsel with him but he proceeded to preach a sermon to the chaplain. About all the help the pastor could offer was to urge him to consult a psychiatrist.)

Fortunately, the nurse apprehended this self-appointed chaplain before he did much damage.

The patient with a heart ailment is usually aware of the nature of the sickness and welcomes the pastor's call. The degree of the patient's apprehensiveness will depend upon a number of factors. The most important of these is the patient's religious beliefs. If he feels that he is reasonably prepared, spiritually, to die, there will not be as much fear as there is when the patient knows that he is not.

If the patient thinks that loved ones have a measure of economic security, this will alleviate that worry. On the other hand, when there are inadequate financial resources, the patient may be considerably concerned about it except when sedated.

The patient's age may also affect his attitude toward imminent death. An aging person who has achieved many of his goals and whose children are mature, while he may not want the end to come, will probably not be as apprehensive about it as a younger person. On the other hand, when a sick person's spouse is feeble and dependent upon him, the patient may worry about this and want to discuss it with the pastor. "She needs me so badly," an elderly man confided to his pastor, "I hope God will let me live so I can take care of her."

In many heart cases there may be periods of apparent improvement. The patient may be permitted to feed himself and sit in a chair for a few minutes each day and the pastor may conclude that the patient is going to recover. However, when the pastor calls the next time, the patient may be much worse. When death comes it will most likely happen suddenly.

Roman Catholic. The Roman Catholic heart patient may be prepared for either life or death by Confession, Holy Communion and Extreme Unction. The latter sacrament may be administered once in any serious illness. If the patient should show improvement, as so often happens with cardiac diseases, Extreme Unction may be repeated when a relapse occurs.

Jewish patients. A prayer that may be used by the rabbi when the patient is seriously sick is the following:[2]

> Hear my voice, O Lord, when I call; be gracious to me and answer me! (Psalm 27:7). O Lord, in whose hand is the soul of every living thing, I turn unto Thee in my distress. Let not despair overwhelm me. Give me patience and faith when the hours are heavy. Renew my trust in Thy mercy and loving kindness. Bless the efforts of my physician and all those who attend me.
>
> O Thou, who art the greatest of all physicians, grant me Thy healing, that in vigor of body and mind, I may return to my loved ones for a life marked by good deeds.   Amen.
>
> > Thou has ever been my help;
> > Cast me not off nor forsake me,
> > O God of my salvation.   Amen.

Protestant reassurances. When the pastor approached the bedside, the dying man attempted feebly to press his hand through the oxygen tent. The pastor helped him by putting his hand under the edge of the tent, gently holding his parishioner's hand as he prayed,

> The Lord is the strength of his people,
> he is the saving refuge of his anointed.
> O save thy people, and bless thy heritage;
> be thou their shepherd, and carry them for ever.
>
> > > *Psalm 28:8–9*

> O Lord, our heavenly Father, Thou hast blest us
> Along life's way until today.
> Humbly we call upon Thee
> To continue to regard us with Thy favor.

---

[2] *Healing Cometh From the Lord*, edited by Rabbi Morris Silverman (Hartford, Conn.: Prayer Book Press Publishers, 1960), p. 3.

We are grateful for all that Thou hast done for us,
Especially we are thankful for Jesus our Saviour,
Through Whom we have forgiveness,
and eternal life.
Help us now to feel in our hearts
Thy forgiving love and healing grace,
That we may not be unduly worried
But put all our trust in Thee.
Whatever may be Thy holy will for us,
We rest our souls in Thee,
O blessed Lord, our Saviour and Redeemer.   Amen.

A few moments later his parishioner expired. When the doctor nodded to the wife that it was over, the pastor prayed with the loved ones, the nurse and the doctor,

Dear Lord, receive now unto Thyself,
The soul of this loved one,
And grant unto him all the blessings
Of the eternal life that Thou hast
Provided for Thy children.
With Thy Holy Spirit, comfort and direct
These loved ones in the days ahead
That they may not sorrow
As those who have no hope
Through Jesus Christ, our Lord.   Amen.

A very old hymn expresses a faith and confidence that will comfort a believer who is facing death and knows it;

My Jesus, as Thou wilt! O may Thy will be mine!
Into Thy hand of love I would my all resign.
Through sorrow or through joy, Conduct me as Thine own;
And help me still to say, "My Lord, Thy will be done."

My Jesus as Thou wilt! Though seen through many a tear
Let not my star of hope Grow dim or disappear.
Since Thou on earth hast wept, And sorrowed oft alone,
If I must weep with Thee, My Lord, Thy will be done.

My Jesus, as Thou wilt! All shall be well for me;
Each changing future scene I gladly trust with Thee.

Straight to my home above I travel calmly on,
And sing, in life or death, "My Lord, Thy will be done."
Benjamin Schmolck, c. 1704
Tr. Jane Laurie Borthwick, 1854

Some appropriate Scripture selections for one who might die momentarily are the following ones.

Surely he has borne our griefs and carried our sorrows; yet we esteemed him stricken, smitten by God, and afflicted. But he was wounded for our transgressions, he was bruised for our iniquities; upon him was the chastisement that made us whole, and with his stripes we are healed.

Isaiah 53:4–5

For a brief moment I forsook you, but with great compassion I will gather you. In overflowing wrath for a moment I hid my face from you, but with everlasting love I will have compassion on you, says the Lord, your Redeemer.

Isaiah 54:7–8

Fear not, for I am with you, be not dismayed, for I am your God; I will strengthen you, I will help you, I will uphold you with my victorious right hand.

Isaiah 41:10

Come to me, all who labor and are heavy-laden, and I will give you rest. Take my yoke upon you, and learn from me; for I am gentle and lowly in heart, and you will find rest for your souls. For my yoke is easy, and my burden is light.

Matthew 11:28–30

Jesus said to them, "I am the bread of life; he who comes to me shall not hunger, and he who believes in me shall never thirst . . . and him who comes to me I will not cast out . . . For this is the will of my Father, that every one who sees the Son and believes in him should have eternal life; and I will raise him up at the last day."

John 6:35, 37, 40

But God shows his love for us in that while we were yet sinners Christ died for us . . . but we also rejoice in God through our Lord Jesus Christ, through whom we have now received our reconciliation.

Romans 5:8, 11

And we know that the Son of God has come and has given us understanding, to know him who is true; and we are in him who is true, in his Son Jesus Christ. This is the true God and eternal life.

I John 5:20

A PRAYER FOR ONE ABOUT TO DIE[3]

I am the resurrection and the life,
He that believeth in me shall never die
But shall have everlasting life.
Eternal Father, we lift up our hearts unto
Thee in the quiet of the evening.
As the birds seek their nests
and children the shelter of home at eventide,
So we come unto Thee and are comforted,
Knowing that underneath are the Everlasting Armes.
Give us rest in the night and in sleep envelop us,
and finally bring us unto eternal life.
Now may the Lord Jesus be and abide with you,
The Lord graciously with His favor look upon
you and give you peace. Through Jesus Christ
our Lord.   Amen.

Another prayer the pastor may want to use as the parishioner is dying is this following one.[4]

Almighty and merciful God and Father! My life draws to a close. Thou art calling me from this earth. Thy will be done. I place myself in Thy hands and rest in Thine eternal love. Graciously didst Thou lead me hitherto. Oh, mercifully con-

---

[3] Russell L. Dicks, *Comfort Ye My People* (New York: The Macmillan Company, 1947), p. 39.

[4] H. J. Schick, *Pastor's Pocket Manual* (St. Louis: Eden Publishing House, 1930), p. 87.

duct me to the heavenly mansions of peace and life eternal. Count not my sins against me: let grace prevail over justice. Grant me pardon and the crown of life for Jesus' sake. Come, heavenly Father; come, Divine Redeemer; come Holy Spirit! I am thine! Into Thy hand I commend my spirit.   Amen.

At the Time of a Fatal Accident

Fatal accidents are unexpected and leave the deceased's family unprepared for the shock. The pastor may learn of the situation in a number of ways. The immediate family may think of the pastor as soon as they learn of the tragedy, unless they are too emotionally disturbed to think of calling anyone. Usually a family friend, distant relative or a member of the congregation will call the minister.

Finding the patient. Regardless of his source of information, it is important that the minister question the informer regarding the patient's whereabouts. The pastor must not assume that the patient is taken to the hospital nearest the scene of the accident, because the patient (if conscious), the family, or the doctor may prefer a certain hospital. If the informer does not know, he may call the patient's home, a neighbor or preferably the hospital where he thinks the injured one would be taken. The clerk in the emergency room will have the information before the attendant at the information desk.

If the patient was killed instantly in the home, the pastor may go there. If the accident was in an industrial plant, office or on the road the chances are that the fatally injured person will be taken to a hospital and pronounced dead on arrival. As long as there is life, the pastor may assume that the injured one is in a hospital and he may go to that institution's emergency department. It is important that he identify himself upon arrival even if he is in clerical garb, for there may be other patients there. The attendant may share information with him that may help in ministering to the patient and his family. While the diagnosis may not be complete, experienced emergency personnel can estimate the patient's condition. The one in charge can also tell the minister where the patient and his family are.

The pastor will have to decide whom he wishes to see first. I would suggest the family for three reasons. They will need the stabilizing influence of his presence. Also it may require some time for him to actually see and talk with the injured one. In addition, he might learn something about the nature of the injury and the condition of the patient.

How he is received by the immediate family will vary with the emotional condition of the loved ones and his previous relation to them. Since this has happened suddenly, the next of kin may be in shock and respond to his questions with a great deal of hesitation. The pastor may construe this to mean that he is not needed. However, the contrary is usually the case if they know him well and have confidence in him.

On the other hand, he may be received with a burst of emotional affection by some who will clasp him in their arms, weeping. Those who need to cry should be permitted to do so, for in a few minutes they usually become more calm.

After the emotional outburst, relatives may become more calm and if the pastor feels that a prayer would be helpful, he may offer one.

A Brief Prayer in an Emergency

Heavenly Father, with Thy Spirit of love,
Strengthen Thy children who call upon Thee.
Help us to put our trust in Thee
That we may be comforted by Thy Presence.
Bless all that is being done
For this loved one to aid the healing forces
According to Thy Holy Will,
Through Jesus Christ, our Saviour.   Amen.

Jewish Prayer in an Emergency

Eternal is Thy power, O Lord, Thou art mighty to save. In loving kindness Thou sustainest the living; in the multitude of Thy mercies, Thou preservest all. Thou upholdest the falling and healest the sick; freest the captives and keepeth faith with Thy children in death as in life. Who is like unto Thee, Almighty God, Author of life and death, Source of salvation? Praise be Thou, O Lord, who hast implanted within us eternal life.[5]

Visiting the injured one. The pastor will probably find the patient surrounded by nurses and at least one physician who will be ministering to the patient's physical needs and, in their concentration, may not pay any attention to him. If so, he may consult with the hospital chaplain.

If the patient is conscious and dying, the doctor will make a place for the pastor beside the bed. It may be necessary for the minister to don a sterile gown and an attendant will help him with it. Otherwise he may approach the patient, who may or may not recognize him, and the pastor may offer sentences of reassurance such as:

"We are thinking of you and remembering you in our prayers that the Lord may be with you."

SCRIPTURE QUOTATIONS

Who shall separate us from the love of Christ? . . . nor anything else in all creation, will be able to separate us from the love of God in Christ Jesus our Lord.

Romans 8:35, 39

The Lord bless you and keep you:
The Lord make his face to shine upon you, and be
gracious to you:
The Lord lift up his countenance upon you,
and give you peace.

Numbers 6:24–26

If the patient is unconscious or anesthetized, the clergyman may wait until the doctor gives him an opportunity to approach.

---

[5] *The Union Prayerbook for Jewish Worship* (Cincinnati: The Central Conference of American Rabbis, 1947), p. 34.

The Roman Catholic priest may administer Extreme Unction. The pastor or rabbi may lay his hand upon the hand or forehead of the parishioner and speak a benediction.

An appropriate prayer, as the patient is dying, is the following one:

O Lord God, our heavenly Father, we beseeech Thee graciously to accept this Thy servant, forgive him (her) all his (her) sins, mercifully defend him (her) in the hour of his (her) death, and grant him (her) everlasting life; through Jesus Christ, Thy Son, our Lord.   Amen.[6]

ROMAN CATHOLIC PRAYER

O God, to whom it peculiarly belongeth to have mercy always and to spare, we humbly beseech Thee in behalf of the soul of Thy servant (N), which Thou hast this day called out of the world, that Thou wouldst not deliver it into the hands of the enemy, nor be unmindful of it unto the end; but command it to be received by Thy holy angels, and conducted to paradise, its true country: that as in Thee it had faith and hope, it may not suffer the pains of hell, but be put in possession of never ending felicity; through our Lord Jesus Christ.[7]

If the patient's condition permits it, he or she may be transferred to either the Intensive Care Unit of the hospital or to another room where the clergyman will have a better opportunity to minister to the parishioner's spiritual needs.

The clergyman may have privacy with the parishioner by identifying himself to the nurse in charge and asking if the curtain might be drawn. The immediate family will probably be in a nearby waiting room and the next of kin may want to be with the pastor when he reads and prays with the loved one.

---

[6] *Book of Worship*, approved by the General Synod of the Evangelical and Reformed Church (Cleveland: Central Publishing House, 1947), p. 284.

[7] Collect Prayer from the Burial Mass in the *Roman Catholic Missal*.

For this reason I bow my knees before the Father, from whom every family in heaven and on earth is named, that according to the riches of his glory he may grant you to be strengthened with might through his Spirit in the inner man, and that Christ may dwell in your hearts through faith; that you, being rooted and grounded in love, may have power to comprehend with all the saints what is the breadth and length and height and depth, and to know the love of Christ which surpasses knowledge, that you may be filled with all the fulness of God.

Ephesians 3:14–19

And the ransomed of the Lord shall return, and come to Zion with singing, with everlasting joy upon their heads; they shall obtain joy and gladness, and sorrow and sighing shall flee away.

Isaiah 35:10

"Let not your hearts be troubled; believe in God, believe also in me. In my Father's house are many rooms; if it were not so, would I have told you that I go to prepare a place for you? And when I go and prepare a place for you, I will come again and will take you to myself, that where I am you may be also."

John 14:1–3

For God so loved the world that he gave his only Son, that whoever believes in him should not perish but have eternal life.

John 3:16

Even though I walk through the valley of the
    shadow of death,
I fear no evil;
for thou art with me;
thy rod and thy staff,
they comfort me.

Psalm 23:4

A Prayer for One Who Is Fatally Injured

O God, who art our refuge and strength, always a present help in time of trouble, be with us now as we come with a concern in our hearts and a prayer on our faltering lips. Bless this Thy disciple in body and spirit, in this moment of stress and strain. Forgive all sins of thought, word, and deed, the good he (she) has left undone, . . . anything that may have been amiss. Bestow thy gift of righteousness by faith in our Lord Jesus, by whom we are saved!

And help us all to walk humbly before Thee all the days of our lives; through Jesus Christ, our Lord.   Amen.

Friedrich Rest

A Prayer for One Who Is Dying of an Injury

O Lord, our blessed Redeemer, hear us now,
And forever, when we turn to Thee;
We need Thy presence and the assurance
That it is in love that Thou dost visit us.
Forgive us wherever we have failed Thee
And accept us as Thine own.
Remove from the mind our worries
As we now put our trust in Thee,
Keep us and our loved ones in Thy care.
Our lives are in Thy hand
Nurtured there by Thy love.
For Thee we live, for Thee we suffer,
For Thee we die,
Thine will we be in life and in death,
Grant us, O Lord, eternal salvation.   Amen.

When the pastor must tell loved ones. When sudden death occurs away from home, the clergyman may be asked to inform the immediate family, particularly the spouse. Some pastors may prefer to take another person along on this sad mission. However, there are disadvantages in having a third person thrust into a very personal and emotionally and spiritually shattering experience. I think it may be better when the pastor does this alone. However, in a military death, the official delegate will probably accompany the pastor to the home.

The pastor should be as thoroughly informed as possible before he goes into the home. Loved ones, especially the spouse, will want to know how it happened, where the body now is, if anything was done to prevent the death and if the dying person gave any significant directions or what was said after it happened.

On the way, the pastor may prepare himself for the difficult task by praying that God will guide him and help him with the right approach and the proper words. He will want to share the sad news in a manner that will impart spiritual strength and courage and not abruptly shock the loved one.

The expression on the pastor's face as he enters the home may give the first impression that his mission is not a pleasant one. He may approach the spouse with the usual exchange of greetings, but with more reserve, being careful to avoid any superficial talk or frivolous manner.

After they are seated, he may begin by saying, "Under ordinary circumstances I look forward to a call in this home," or, "I wish this visit could be as pleasant as those I have experienced here previously," or if it is the first visit in the home he may say, "I had hoped that my first visit here might be more pleasant than this one."

Any statement that leaves the impression that the pastor is not the harbinger of good news will help prepare the loved one for what is yet to come.

"Why, Reverend is there anything wrong?" Mrs. E asked, surmising from his attitude that there was something amiss.

"I am sorry to say that there is, Helen," he said, using her first name as he always did.

"What is it, Reverend?" she asked, realizing that he was withholding information. "Has anything serious happened to anyone I know?"

"I am sorry to say that it has," he answered.

"To my husband?" she asked. "Has he been in an accident?"

"I was asked to come and tell you that he was injured in an accident," he replied with kindness.

"Tell me about it. Is he badly hurt? Where is he? Did you see him?" she asked, realizing that something very serious had happened to her husband.

"I have not seen him, Helen," he explained. "Mr. Jones called me and said that the accident occurred on the corner of _____ and they rushed him to the hospital. I will take you there if you can go."

"Is he dead?" she asked.

"He has been very badly injured," he said.

"Oh, no, no, no, it can't be," she sobbed. "I know he is dead and you don't want to tell me. I just can't believe it. Will you take me to him?"

"I'll take you to the hospital, Helen," he said, "and I will try to help you all I can. But let me call your sister and ask her to meet us there."

The minister called her sister and told her that Mr. E was injured and asked her to meet them at the emergency department. He did not tell her sister that Mr. E was dead.

Arriving at the hospital, Mrs. E insisted that she wanted to see her husband. The minister stood with her in the treatment room as she gave vent to her feelings of shock and sorrow. Then the pastor said, "Would it be helpful to you if we prayed at this time?"

She nodded her assent and he spoke a prayer.

A Prayer With a Loved One at the Bedside of One Who Died Suddenly

O Blessed God and Father,
We realize that there is but a step
Between us and death,
And that death is not the end of life.
As we pause here in deep reverence,
We thank Thee for our faith and confidence.
Receive our loved one and embrace him
In Thy everlasting arms of love.

For ourselves we pray Thee,
Keep our faith strong,
Grant the courage that we need,
And help us to feel that
We are never alone
For Thou art with us.
Now, O Lord, bestow within us
The inner strength of that peace
That passes all human understanding,
Through our blessed Lord and Redeemer.   Amen.

Next the police and the coroner explained what had happened. The pastor remained as the wife decided which mortician the nurse should contact. It was decided that the mortician would see her in her home. Then the minister assured her that he would call again later in the day, and her sister took her home.

It may seem cruel at first to withhold information as this pastor did, but in doing so he gave her some time to adjust to the terribly disturbing news. To have told her suddenly would have most likely resulted in shock for Mrs. E. He tried to lead her more slowly to a realization of what had happened.

When many people are fatally injured.   Certain catastrophes such as an explosion, a fire, an avalanche, a hurricane, a cyclone, a railroad or airplane accident, a building falling or the explosion of a bomb may cause any number of people to be fatally injured at one time.

Railroad and airplane accidents usually injure people who are not known locally and responsibility for the spiritual welfare of the dying people usually rests upon the hospital chaplains. However, when and where there are no chaplains available, the local clergy will need to minister to the spiritual needs of the victims.

It would be very confusing amid the turmoil if all the local clergy rushed to the scene of the accident. Therefore, it is advisable for the ministers' association to formulate a plan whereby designated clergy would minister to the spiritual needs when many unknown people are fatally injured.

With the ever-present threat of war, local clergy will also

want to cooperate with civic and health authorities in each city or community to devise a workable method whereby fatally injured people might receive spiritual aid.

The role of the Roman Catholic priest is rather clearly defined when he knows, usually by the medal carried or worn on the body, that the dying or dead person is of the Roman Catholic faith.

In practice, persons who have died suddenly can be anointed as much as two or three hours after death. If these people have died violently in accidents, however, and the bodies are notably dismembered, crushed, mutilated, or burned, perhaps not more than thirty minutes should be allowed, for it is evident that in these cases death follows rapidly upon the traumatic event.[8]

The Roman Catholic priest may also minister to Protestants:

Heretics and such Protestants as are in good faith who belong to a religious group that admits the sacrament of penance, can be absolved conditionally after they lose consciousness. Protestants cannot be absolved if they positively reject the sacrament, or even negatively know nothing about it; such persons have no intention of receiving absolution. They do not have the habitual implicit intention of doing so, and, on the contrary, have the habitual tendency of not receiving it. Those who know nothing about the sacrament have no intention one way or another.[9]

Remember, all that has been written about dying people's thoughts has been expressed by persons who are living, including those who presume to prescribe a ministry to the spiritual needs of the dying. After many years of ministry to dying people it is my opinion that when the end of earthly life draws near, most people appreciate the presence and the words of a man of God, whether minister, priest or rabbi.

---

[8] Patrick O'Brian, C. M., *A Handbook for Hospital Chaplains* (St. Louis and London: B. Herder Book Co., 1959), p. 251.

[9] *Ibid.*, p. 248.

Certainly, every Protestant, Roman Catholic and Jew would prefer his own clergyman, but when death is imminent, earthly distinctions are really not very important to most believers. The important consideration is eternal salvation and most people know that God is not sectarian and the prayers of all sincere people are heard by Him.

The Protestant ministry in an emergency.   In an emergency situation, Protestant clergy should be prepared to administer Baptism, Holy Communion and the rite of anointing. When time is of the essence, the pastor may need to improvise brief rituals for emergency situations and conditional baptism. Suggested forms are in the last chapter of this book.

BRIEF PRAYERS FOR THE DYING

Our heavenly Father, look with Thy favor upon this Thy servant. Forgive all his (her) sins; grant him (her) salvation both now and in the eternal life; through Jesus Christ, our Lord.   Amen.

Defend, O Lord, this Thy servant with Thy heavenly grace; that he (she) may continue Thine forever; and daily increase in Thy Holy Spirit, until he (she) come to Thy everlasting kingdom.   Amen.[10]

O Lord God, our heavenly Father, we beseech Thee graciously to accept this Thy servant, forgive him (her) all his (her) sins, mercifully defend him (her) in the hour of death, and grant him (her) everlasting life; through Jesus Christ, Thy Son, our Saviour.   Amen.[11]

NUNC DIMITTIS

Lord, now lettest Thou Thy servant depart in peace: According to Thy word; For mine eyes have seen Thy salvation: which Thou hast prepared before the face of all people; A

---

[10] *Book of Worship,* approved by the General Synod of the Evangelical and Reformed Church, 1947, p. 102.
[11] *Ibid.,* p. 284.

light to lighten the Gentiles; And the glory of Thy people Israel.[12]

AGNUS DEI

O Christ, Thou Lamb of God, that takest away the sin of the world, have mercy upon us. O Christ, Thou Lamb of God, that takest away the sin of the world, have mercy upon us. O Christ, Thou Lamb of God, that takest away the sin of the world, grant us Thy peace.   Amen.[13]

WHEN THE SOUL HAS TAKEN ITS LEAVE

Into Thy loving care, O blessed Savior
We commend the soul of Thy servant.
Receive him (her) we beseech Thee,
With mercy forgive all his (her) sins,
And grant him (her) a safe place
In Thy house of many mansions,
There to dwell in rest and peace
Praising Thy Holy Name in all eternity.   Amen.

When One Commits Suicide

"Would you want to talk with me about it?" her pastor asked Mrs. F kindly, while she was yet conscious.

She was about forty-five years old. Her only daughter was married. The pastor knew that her marriage had weathered some serious storms, for on two occasions her husband had left her. But, each time they had reconciled. On one occasion Mr. F had told him that she was inordinately jealous, that he could not even look at another woman "without hearing about it forever." He claimed that he gave her no reasons to doubt his fidelity; however, she maintained that he did. The couple's married daughter told the pastor that her mother had mentioned suicide on one occasion, but no one took the threat seriously. At the time of her attempt, her husband had left her again.

---

[12] *Ibid.*, p. 285.
[13] *Ibid.*, p. 284.

"Pray that God will forgive me," she replied to the pastor's question. He had to listen closely for she could scarcely speak. Undoubtedly her throat was burned by the poison she drank. A neighbor, knowing Mrs. F to be alone in the home, became suspicious and went to see her. She found and rushed her to a hospital, but it was too late to save her life.

"I will pray with you," he said kindly, "for I know you need God's help now."

"I couldn't help it, Reverend," she managed to say, "I would rather be dead. No one cares."

Her daughter arrived at that moment, and rushing by the pastor, hugged and kissed her mother. Sobbing, she repeated, "Why did you do it? Oh, why did you do it?"

Tears trickled down the mother's cheeks but she did not reply. Giving the daughter a few moments to compose herself, the pastor said, "Your mother would like me to pray with her. Will you join us in our prayers?"

Mrs. F weakly folded her hands, as did the daughter, and the pastor prayed:

> Our heavenly Father, Thou dost understand us far better than we know ourselves. In the time of stress when we are bewildered we may do things we sincerely regret. Look with forgiving mercy upon this Thy child and forgive all her sins. Accept her sincere repentance and now strengthen her faith in Thee. Whatever may be Thy holy will regarding her earthly life, we trust in Thy divine wisdom and love. We know that Thou dost love us and we turn to Thee in confidence. Bless us now and evermore with Thy Presence through Jesus Christ, our Lord. Amen.

"Thank you, Reverend," she whispered.

"Momma thinks that no one loves her," the daughter sobbed, "but we do."

The pastor turned and saw Mr. F approaching the bed. Bewildered, he stood looking at her a moment, then leaned over and put his face beside hers as he held her hand. She responded by moving her other hand as if to embrace him. Thereafter she lapsed into unconsciousness and passed away a day later.

In conversation with Mr. F, he explained that Mrs. F was an illegitimate child, shunted from one relative to another. She had been a loving wife but nagged and was very jealous to the extent that their life together was one unhappy episode after another. The incident that caused him to leave her this last time was the result of an entirely innocent occurrence. A woman who worked with Mr. F told him that her husband was having trouble with their car. She asked Mr. F to take her home, since it was not out of his way to do so.

Thinking nothing of it, he took her home and tarried for about a half-hour talking with her husband as he tried to get the car started. When he arrived at his home Mrs. F was in a rage. A woman had called to tell her that she saw her husband with another woman in his car. She raised such a "storm" over it that he gathered a few of his belongings and went to his mother's home again. The neighbor who found Mrs. F called him at the factory and informed the daughter.

The causes of suicide have been studied through the years. There is no simple answer. Many factors may cause feelings of utter despair. Mrs. F, most likely, could have been helped if she had received psychiatric treatment. Her talk of suicide should not have been taken lightly.

The church, Christian and Jewish, has stood adamantly on its position that suicide is a transgression of the commandment, "Thou shalt not kill." However, there are some conditions under which the church believes that God will extend forgiveness.

The Roman Catholic view. The Roman Catholic Church maintains that all life is sacred including that of animals. To kill or injure animals without good reason is considered sinful, but not a violation of the commandment.[14]

---

[14] Rev. John A. O'Brien, Ph.D., *The Catholic Faith, An Official edition of the Revised Baltimore Catechism No. 3.* (Notre Dame: Ave Maria Press, 1954), p. 164.

It is also a law of the church that the bodies of those who have knowingly and deliberately committed suicide shall not be given a Christian burial.[15]

The phrase "knowingly and deliberately" is vitally important. You will recall that Mrs. F said, "I couldn't help it. I would rather be dead. No one cares." Her statement clearly indicated that she was forcefully impelled by emotional stresses that were beyond her ability to control.

The Roman Catholic priest's ministry to a parishioner who has committed suicide will depend upon the person's former faithfulness and if he thinks that this was done during a temporary lapse of reason. He can administer the sacraments, conditionally, in almost any circumstances for the benefit of the dying. When in doubt he may consult the Bishop.

Jewish views. Jewish religious philosophy stresses the sacredness of human life. Man is now living without his consent and will have to die without his approval. And, without his consent he will have to render account for his life before the supreme King, the holy One, blessed be He.[16]

As a basic principle and practice of the Jewish faith, suicide is prohibited. The giving and taking of human life is only God's prerogative. If it happens and the rabbi has valid reasons to believe that the person was mentally ill and it was done without malice aforethought, then he may minister to the dying one as he would to any other sick person.

Protestant views. Among Protestants there seems to be a unanimity of belief that human life is sacred and that suicide is a transgression of God's commandment.

"I think that a person who commits suicide must be mentally ill when he does it," one pastor said, "and I would minister to him as I would to any parishioner dying of another disease."

"If the local church has an ordinance forbidding a church

---

[15] *Ibid.,* p. 165.
[16] *The Union Prayerbook for Jewish Worship* (Cincinnati: The Central Conference of American Rabbis, 1947), p. 174.

funeral for a victim of suicide," another pastor said, "I suppose I would have to abide by it, but I would not like it. I would minister to the dying patient as I would to any other Christian. But I would certainly try to help the dying one find peace with God."

"If we say that we have no sin, we deceive ourselves and the truth is not in us," another pastor said. "We have all transgressed God's commandments and need the redeeming grace of our Lord to stand in the presence of God. To take one's own life is a sin, unless the person is driven to it beyond his ability to resist. Then, he must depend upon God's mercy and love."

Most Protestants regard the act as sinful unless the individual is not responsible for his action. Still, it must be remembered that God alone is the judge, and Protestants, Roman Catholics and Jews teach that God forgives sin. A person who dies by suicide may find forgiveness, for only God knows the motives and the attitude of the dying one.

In our society, suicide is taboo. It may be tolerated by some when the victim is incurably ill or despondent. Even then, the family will be plagued with strong feelings of shame and guilt.

They may think, and sometimes rightfully so, that they contributed to the despondency of the dying one. Mr. F, no doubt, will always feel that he contributed to her act by leaving her. The daughter will be plagued with misgivings regarding her attitude toward her mother. Actually, the gossipy friend who telephoned Mrs. F was immediately responsible for her death. The pastor will need to help both husband and daughter find peace through sincere repentance and faith.

In almost every instance, the pastor, priest or rabbi will need to minister to members of the family of the dying person in the area of guilt and misgivings.

Scripture selections the pastor may find to be helpful to the dying person follow:

The Lord is merciful and gracious,
slow to anger and abounding in steadfast love.
He will not always chide,
nor will he keep his anger for ever.

He does not deal with us according to our sins,
nor requite us according to our iniquities.
For as the heavens are high above the earth,
so great is his steadfast love toward those
who fear him;
as far as the east is from the west,
so far does he remove our transgressions from us.

Psalm 103:8–12

Turn thou to me, and be gracious to me;
for I am lonely and afflicted.
Relieve the troubles of my heart,
and bring me out of my distresses.
Consider my affliction and my trouble,
and forgive all my sins.

Psalm 25:16–18

If we confess our sins, he is faithful and just, and will forgive
our sins and cleanse us from all unrighteousness.

I John 1:9

. . . "I will never fail you nor forsake you." Hence we
can confidently say,
"The Lord is my helper,
I will not be afraid;
what can man do to me?"

Hebrews 13:5, 6

But he said to me, "My grace is sufficient for you, for my
power is made perfect in weakness."

II Corinthians 12:9

So you have sorrow now, but I will see you again and your
hearts will rejoice, and no one will take your joy from you.

John 16:22

Peace I leave with you; my peace I give to you; not as the
world gives do I give to you. Let not your hearts be troubled,
neither let them be afraid.

John 14:27

The Kyrie

Lord, have mercy upon us,
Christ, have mercy upon us,
Lord, have mercy upon us.

A Prayer of Repentance

Dear Father in heaven,
Look with mercy upon us,
For in our anguish we turn to Thee.
We are heartily sorry for our sins,
And therefore deal not with us
According to our iniquities.
Remember, O Lord, that we are mortal;
Look into our hearts,
Regard in love our sincere repentance,
Our mixed emotions,
Our tangled thoughts,
And for Jesus' sake forgive us.
Grant us now Thy peace,
And may we find our rest in Thee
Now and evermore.   Amen.

An Assurance of Pardon

Almighty God, unto whom all hearts are open, all desires
known, and from whom no secrets are hid, cleanse the
thought of our hearts by the inspiration of Thy Holy Spirit,
that we may perfectly love Thee, and worthily magnify Thy
Holy Name; through Jesus Christ our Lord.   Amen.

Words of Absolution

Hearken now unto the comforting assurance of the grace of
God, promised in the Gospel to all that repent and believe:
As I live, saith the Lord God, I have no pleasure in the death
of the wicked, but that the wicked turn from his way and
live.

Unto you, therefore, who truly repent and believe in

the Lord Jesus Christ, with full purpose of new obedience, I announce and declare, by the authority and in the Name of Christ, that your sins are forgiven, according to His promise in the Gospel; through Jesus Christ our Lord.   Amen.

After the person has deceased the pastor may offer a prayer with the loved ones at the bedside.

A Prayer After the Patient Has Deceased

Dear God and Father, who has redeemed us;
Keep this, our loved one in Thy eternal care,
And grant him (her) release from all burdens
That he (she) may find bliss and joy with Thee.
Look with favor upon these loved ones,
Strengthen and guide and comfort them.
May they feel the nearness of Thy Presence
As they look with faith to the days ahead.
And when our earthly tasks are done,
Grant us a holy rest, and peace at last,
Through Jesus Christ, our Lord.   Amen.

A Lutheran Prayer[17]

When the circumstances are such as to make it possible for a Christian minister to officiate at the burial of a suicide this prayer may be used. (Author's note: It could also be used in the presence of loved ones at the bedside of one who has deceased.)

Merciful God and Father, how unsearchable are Thy judgments, and Thy ways past finding out. We are troubled, yet not distressed; we are perplexed, but not in despair; cast down, but not destroyed. Thou, O Lord, knowest our frame; Thou rememberest that we are but dust. The foolish things of this world and the weak and base things which are despised hast Thou chosen; that no flesh may glory in Thy sight. Thy strength is made perfect in weakness, and Thy grace in Christ Jesus is sufficient unto us. We pray Thee,

---

[17] *The Lutheran Agenda* (St. Louis: Concordia Publishing House, n. d.), p. 103.

grant us grace to make diligent use of Thy Word and Sacrament that we may have the needful strength to resist the wiles of the evil Foe, who seeks to destroy our souls and minds and bodies. Let us never boast of our strength, but ever be mindful of Thy Word. Let him that thinketh he standeth take heed lest he fall. With deep humility we bow before Thee in this hour in which our hearts are burdened with sorrow and grief. We yield ourselves to Thy fatherly guidance with childlike confidence. Thou wilt lead us with Thy right hand and finally receive us unto glory for the sake of Jesus Christ, our only Mediator and Redeemer.   Amen.

When One Is an Unbeliever

Mr. G was about 75 years old. He once owned a business (selling tombstones) and as long as he was able to do so, he visited it. He liked to carve a stone.

His wife was a Christian and attended worship quite regularly until recent years. She had to find transportation or walk to church because Mr. G would not drive her there in their old car. The minister had seen him once at the place of business and another time in the home, but he was always very curt with the pastor. Someone told the minister that Mr. G was an unbeliever.

When Mr. G became seriously ill he refused to go to a hospital and remained in his home. His wife sent word to the pastor and asked him to call.

The first call.   When the minister came into the bedroom, led by Mrs. G, she said, "Henry, the minister is here."

He: He don't have to come to see me.
Pastor: That's right, I don't. I just wanted to see how you are getting along.
He: I'm not very well, I guess you can see that.
Pastor: Have you been sick very long?
He: I don't know why you're askin' those questions.

Pastor: Because I'm interested in you.

He: Well, you needn't be. [Turning to Mrs. G] Get me a drink of water. [She leaves]

Pastor: I take it, Mr. G, you'd rather I don't visit you.

He: You can visit all you want to, but don't talk to me about religion. I've got along in life without God, if there is one, and I don't intend to change before I die.

Pastor: You mean you don't believe in God?

He: There ain't no God.

Pastor: I had hoped my visit would be welcome and helpful to you. I am interested in your welfare in this world and in the eternal life.

He: You can quit being interested 'cause there ain't no eternal life. Anyway, when I die, I'll be dead and that'll be the end of it.

Mrs. G handed him a glass of water. He tasted it and before she could step aside he threw the rest of the contents of the glass in her face.

He: That water's too warm. Here, take this and get me a glass of cold water.

This demonstration caused the pastor to realize that Mr. G was not only sick but emotionally irresponsible as well. He thought to scold him for his crudeness, but he held his tongue.

Pastor: Where were you born and raised, Mr. G?

He: I was born over in Pennsylvania, in the hills. That's where I learned to work with stone. All other materials rot sooner or later, but stone never does. It lasts; yes, sir, it lasts forever.

Pastor: So you spent your life making things that are going to last a lot longer than you or I are.

He: I've worked with only the best stone.

Mrs. G returned with a glass of water.
He drank the water and handed the glass to her.

He: Now, thank you for the visit.

The pastor arose saying, "Good-by, Mr. G," but there was no response. Mrs. G went with him to the front door.

She: I'm sorry he was so ugly to you, Reverend.
Pastor: Think nothing of it.
She: I guess you won't want to come back.
Pastor: I will be pleased to come again if you would like for me to.
She: Please do and remember him in your prayers. I am so worried about him. He wasn't always as mean as he is now, but he never would believe in God. At least he always says that.

In trying to evaluate his call the pastor realized that he had not made contact with Mr. G. He had to use considerable self-control when Mr. G threw the water in Mrs. G's face. He thought by asking him about his life Mr. G might become more friendly and that he might find some clue that would help him understand Mr. G's attitude. Mr. G would talk only about stone and when he thought the pastor might argue with him, he invited him to leave. Mrs. G's words that he had not always been so mean are significant.

Second call.   It was about six days later. Mr. G was lying on a couch in the living room. He was noticeably thinner and not shaved. Mrs. G answered his knock on the door and when he came in, Mr. G turned his face to the wall.

Pastor: Good afternoon, Mr. G.
She: Won't you be seated?
Pastor: Thank you.
She: It's nice weather we're having. I think Henry is a little better this afternoon.
Pastor: Are you feeling better, Mr. G?
He: I guess you can see that I ain't no better and I don't think I'll ever be.

Pastor: What makes you think that?

He: The way I feel, of course. Every man's got to die sometime.

Pastor: Have you been thinking about dying?

He: If I ain't ready now, I never will be.

Pastor: Have you prayed about it?

He: Why should I? I don't talk to myself.

Pastor: I see that you would rather not talk about anything spiritual, but I will think of you in my prayers.

He: When I die, Reverend, I don't want you saying any prayers over me.

Pastor: What gives you the idea that I will?

He: I know she'll want you to, so I'm tellin' you right now.

Pastor: When I conduct a funeral, Mr. G, I do it for the living. It will be too late for you to do any praying then, so it will be for those who want it and are helped by it. And as long as you are living, I'm going to keep on praying for you.

He: That's up to you.

Pastor: Good-by, Mr. G.

He: Good-by.

Mrs. G went with him out on the porch closing the door behind her. "It's no use, Reverend," she said sadly. "Nothing will ever change him."

"You are probably right," the pastor said. "Maybe we are trying too hard. But there's nothing that can keep us from loving him and praying for him."

Third call. Mr. G was in bed again, very weak, his breathing labored, his whiskers long. He was very thin.

"Good afternoon, Mr. G," the pastor greeted him. Mr. G turned toward him and seemed to acknowledge his presence with his eyes.

Pastor: Would you like for me to sit a few moments here with you?

He: You can if you want to.

Pastor: I just want you to know that as a Christian I love you and God loves you, too.

He: Uh huh.

Pastor: There must have been some experience in your life that turned you against God, but He understands and loves you just the same.

He: That's over with now. Bygones is bygones.

Pastor: I wish you would let me help you with whatever it was.

He: I don't want to talk about it.

Pastor: Is there anything you want to talk about?

He: Nothin' that I know of.

Pastor: May I ask you once more: Would you want me to pray with you?

He: I don't want you or anybody to pray with me.

Pastor: Then I'll be going. Good-by and God bless you.

He: Good-by.

In the living room, the pastor asked Mrs. G if she would want him to pray with her.

"Please do, Reverend," she said, "and remember Henry in your prayer."

THE PASTOR'S PRAYER

Our heavenly Father, we turn to Thee with all that lies upon our hearts. In these moments we think of Henry whom Thou dost love. Only Thou canst understand what has turned him against Thee. Thou art long-suffering and kind and full of wisdom. Somehow come into his life that he might know the comfort of Thy Presence and feel Thy forgiving love. Wouldst Thou continue to bless Mrs. G with inner strength, faith, courage and love and hear her prayers, through Jesus Christ our Lord.   Amen.

Fourth call.   Mr. G was very "low" and did not respond to the pastor's words at all. The minister brought Mrs. G the comfort of some passages of Scripture and prayer. If Mr. G heard any of it, he gave no indication.

A few days later he passed away. The pastor conducted a Christian service as he told Mr. G that he would. Since there were no children, he drove to the home after the funeral. Another lady, evidently a distant relative, was there with Mrs. G who expressed a desire to see the stone her husband had reserved for himself. The pastor took them in his car. The new owner guided them to the stone. It was of medium size, of the best marble, highly polished. On one side was Mr. G's birth date, on the other, his wife's. Between the two inscriptions he had carved a hand with the index finger pointing skyward.

Clergymen aren't called upon by many unbelievers, because they usually remain outside the church. It is commonly accepted that they almost always change their attitude before dying. Some do. As a hospital chaplain, I minister to many people who have no church affiliation, but that does not necessarily indicate disbelief in God.

Some people give the impression that they are unbelievers when they are not. They may not accept certain beliefs that some may regard as essential to salvation. If church membership is one of them, then the pastor will minister to many dying people in that category.

Where atheism exists, the pastor looks for some personal experience that has precipitated this attitude. If he establishes rapport, he may find the cause and then be in a better position to assist the dying one into a spiritual attitude of faith that accepts and longs for God's grace and love.

In Mr. G's case, the pastor did not gain his confidence. Perhaps he was trying too hard. Mrs. G's observation that Mr. G had not always been so mean indicated that the sickness and/or the medication may have affected his personality.

The carved hand pointing heavenward on his tombstone may indicate that Mr. G harbored some beliefs about God and immortality that he consciously tried to repress. This brought a small measure of comfort to Mrs. G.

Careless unbelief.   Mr. H, 36, was seriously injured in an auto accident and rushed to the hospital. He was conscious. From him the emergency staff learned his name and a few other essential facts. His wife, who lived in a distant city, was being notified when the chaplain arrived.

Doctor: Harold, this is the hospital chaplain who will talk with you.

Chaplain: We want you to know that you are with people who will help you. As a minister, I'll assist you all that I can. In order to minister to your spiritual needs properly, will you tell us if you are Protestant, Catholic or Jewish.

Harold: I'm nothing.

Doctor: I suggest you start being something now, Harold, because you're seriously hurt.

Harold: [No response]

Chaplain: We'll think of you in our prayers.

Nurse: Why don't you pray for him now?

Chaplain: If Harold has no objections. Would you like us to pray?

Harold: I have no objections.

[The chaplain spoke a prayer imploring God's mercy and His healing forces in Harold's behalf.]

Doctor: Thank you, chaplain. Stay around a while if you can.

Harold: Thanks.

He was taken to surgery. Thereafter the chaplain visited him often. Slowly, Harold recovered. He seemed to welcome the chaplain's calls and they became friends. The chaplain often talked with Mrs. H, too. In their talks, the chaplain learned, that Harold was a successful salesman, but the family lived beyond his means. They had two children, a son, 11, and a daughter, 9. The children did not attend Sunday school.

He and Mrs. H spent a lot of money entertaining their social set and considered themselves to be sophisticated. At their parties they drank quite a bit. With the exception of two Roman Catholic couples, none of their group belonged to any church. He and his wife had not been in a church in many years.

Harold said that he was not an atheist; he just did not bother thinking about religion at all. That is the reason he said he was "nothing" in the emergency room.

Chaplain: Do you now think that this is really the way you want to continue living your life?

Harold: I've had a lot of time to do some thinking.

Chaplain: I've often wondered what you thought after you realized that you were so badly hurt.

Harold: It was a funny feeling. I knew I'd have to stop kidding myself. If there is a God I'd look mighty silly. I wasn't always like this. My mother was a Christian woman and sent me to Sunday school. But in my teens I got away from it. In college I never went to church. Some of the professors even made snide remarks about religion. But, we were married in a church, where her folks belonged. It was a big wedding. After that I was on the road so much, I just forgot all about religion. I can't say that I was really much afraid; I guess I was stunned. I didn't know what to think.

Chaplain: If I understand you, you're saying that you just became a careless unbeliever, is that right?

Harold: You might call it that.

Chaplain: The important thing is how you feel about it now.

Harold: I've had a mighty close call and I'm thankful that I'm alive.

Chaplain: As you say, you have a lot of people to thank for that. Do you think that perhaps God also wants you to get well?

Harold: I've been thinking about that. I'll have to make some adjustments in my living habits and thinking. And don't forget, I have a family, too.

Chaplain: You might as well also include your social as-

sociates. What will they think and say if you return as a person with religious thoughts?

Harold: I have an idea that some of them are fed up
with the way we are living, anyway.

Chaplain: If you would like me to, I will contact the pastor
of a church in your vicinity and ask him to visit
you and your family when you return home.

After much discussion Harold was quite certain that he
knew the name of a church near their home, and the chaplain
contacted the pastor.

During the long period of convalescence, the chaplain read
many Scripture selections to Harold. Some of them are the following:

SCRIPTURES FOR A CARELESS UNBELIEVER

And God spoke all these words, saying, "I am the Lord
your God, who brought you out of the land of Egypt, out
of the house of bondage.

"You shall have no other gods before me.

"You shall not make yourself a graven image, or any like-
ness of anything that is in heaven above, or that is in the
earth beneath, or that is in the water under the earth; you
shall not bow down to them or serve them; for I the Lord
your God am a jealous God, visiting the iniquity of the
fathers upon the children to the third and the fourth generation of those who hate me, but showing steadfast love to
thousands of those who love me and keep my commandments.

"You shall not take the name of the Lord your God in vain;
for the Lord will not hold him guiltless who takes his name
in vain.

"Remember the sabbath day, to keep it holy. Six days you
shall labor, and do all your work; but the seventh day is a
sabbath to the Lord your God; in it you shall not do any

work, you, or your son, or your daughter, your manservant, or your maidservant, or your cattle, or the sojourner who is within your gates; for in six days the Lord made heaven and earth, the sea, and all that is in them, and rested the seventh day; therefore the Lord blessed the sabbath day and hallowed it.

"Honor your father and your mother, that your days may be long in the land which the Lord your God gives you.

"You shall not kill.

"You shall not commit adultery.

"You shall not steal.

"You shall not bear false witness against your neighbor.

"You shall not covet your neighbor's house; you shall not covet your neighbor's wife, or his manservant, or his maidservant, or his ox, or his ass, or anything that is your neighbor's."

Exodus 20:1–17

He said to him, "What is written in the law? How do you read?" And he answered, "You shall love the Lord your God with all your heart, and with all your soul, and with all your strength, and with all your mind; and your neighbor as yourself." And he said to him, "You have answered right; do this, and you will live."

Luke 10:26–28

But when the time had fully come, God sent forth his Son, born of woman, born under the law, to redeem those who were under the law, so that we might receive adoption as sons.

Galatians 4:4–5

For in him the whole fulness of deity dwells bodily, and you have come to fulness of life in him, who is the head of all rule and authority.

Colossians 2:9–10

You know that you were ransomed from the futile ways inherited from your fathers, not with perishable things such as silver or gold, but with the precious blood of Christ, like that of a lamb without blemish or spot.

I Peter 1:18–19

So every one who acknowledges me before men, I also will acknowledge before my Father who is in heaven.

Matthew 10:32

. . . "Believe in the Lord Jesus, and you will be saved, you and your household."

Acts 16:31

Prayer for a Very Sick Careless Unbeliever

O Lord, our God, we turn to Thee,
In Thy holy word Thou hast assured us
That though the mountains should depart
And the hills be removed,
Thy kindness shall not depart from us.
O most faithful Father, we did forget Thee,
And neglect Thy holy commandments,
And sin against Thee by thought, word and deed;
Yet Thou didst not forget us,
But didst graciously wait upon us.
We pray Thee; have mercy,
Comfort our hearts with the assurance
That in sickness and distress
We can still turn to Thee and pray
That Thou wouldst receive us
And accept our humble repentance.
Thou art Life, Light and Love,
Let this be our comfort in life and death,
Through Jesus Christ, our Saviour.   Amen.

Prayer at the Bedside of a Dying Unbeliever

Lord God, our heavenly Father, Thou art Light
And in Thee there is no darkness at all;
Thou knowest our frame,

Thou rememberest that we are dust.
Look Thou with understanding love
Upon us and especially our loved one
Who is about (has) to depart (departed) this life.
We are strongly tied with the bonds of love,
Hear our prayers and consider our thoughts.
Grant, O Lord, that even in these moments
He (she) may turn to Thee
And accept the love Thou dost extend,
Either consciously or in Thy eternal Presence,
Through Jesus Christ, our blessed Redeemer.   Amen.

CHAPTER FIVE

SITUATIONS
ACCORDING To AGE

How to Work With the Physician

Both the pastor and the physician can be more helpful to a dying patient and his family when rapport exists between them. The patient and the loved ones need the support of both and when there is mutual respect between them, their attitude emanates confidence, faith and understanding.

You will recall that in the case of Mr. H, the physician and the nurse were concerned about the patient's spiritual welfare. Doctors and nurses do not consider themselves to be adequately prepared to meet the spiritual needs of the patient any more than the clergyman considers himself adequate to the medical needs of one who is sick. However, doctors and nurses do the best that they can when a clergyman is not available.

In the emergency room the doctor said to the chaplain, "Stay around awhile if you can." If Mr. H's condition had become worse and he could not have survived surgery, the doctor would have expected the chaplain to "prepare him to die."

When the pastor thinks that his ministry to the dying person will be more effective if he has more information about the physical or emotional condition of the patient, he may consult the physician.

As an illustration, Mr. I had a severely injured leg that had to be amputated. He had been a faithful member of the church, taught the men's Bible class and was very friendly with the pastor. During the first few calls Mr. I appreciated the pastor's prayers. Then, abruptly, his attitude changed. He told the pastor not

to pray with him and talked disparagingly about his wife and everyone in general. He was not himself.

The pastor was puzzled until he happened to meet Mr. I's physician. The doctor explained that the patient's personality change was due to a temporary toxic condition. He also told the pastor to comfort Mrs. I with the assurance that her husband was not himself and probably would not even remember what he said and did during this period. With this knowledge the pastor could be more helpful to both.

When the pastor is puzzled about a patient's personality change, the physician can tell him whether the condition is pathological.

The prognosis may also help the pastor in offering guidance to the patient's loved ones. How long will the patient live? Should the patient be returned to the home to die? How much care will be involved before the end comes? The physician can help the pastor with all of these questions.

The patient who develops spiritual problems often reveals them to the physician first. The patient hesitates to speak to his pastor, lest he react with a show of disappointment. On many occasions both doctors and nurses have called my attention to patients with spiritual problems. In each case, I encourage the troubled one to confide in his or her clergyman.

The physician expects the clergyman to be adequately prepared to meet the patient's spiritual needs. He does not like an unskilled minister to further confuse or disturb the dying one.

Mutual Confidence and Respect

The physician expects the pastor to regard conversations about the patient's condition as confidential. If the pastor thinks the patient should know the physician has shared some information with him, he must have the doctor's permission before talking to the patient.

In a like manner, the pastor expects the physician to be ethical in his relationship with him. Most physicians observe a very strict code of eithics in that respect.

The Death of a Child

A pastor's ministry to a dying child is greatly influenced by the patient's age. In the case of an infant, ministry will be to members of the family. The parents may want the child baptized if this is in accord with their beliefs. Where infant baptism is not practiced, it may help if the pastor places his hand upon the little one's forehead and blesses it.

BLESSING FOR A DYING INFANT

Our Lord and Saviour, Thou didst take little children in Thy arms and bless them. Comfort this precious one in the arms of Thy compassion. Bless, preserve and keep him (her) and grant unto this Thy child complete contentment and security in Thy Love.   Amen.

After the child has expired. To spiritually support the loved ones after the child has expired the minister may quote comforting passages from the Scriptures.

He will feed his flock like a shepherd, he will gather the lambs in his arms, he will carry them in his bosom, and gently lead those that are with young.

Isaiah 40:11

Jesus said, "Let the children come to me, and do not hinder them; for to such belongs the kingdom of heaven."

Matthew 19:14

And he took them in his arms and blessed them, laying his hands upon them.

Mark 10:16

Therefore are they before the throne of God, and serve him day and night within his temple; and he who sits upon the throne will shelter them with his presence.

They shall hunger no more, neither thirst any more; the sun shall not strike them, nor any scorching heat. For the

Lamb in the midst of the throne will be their shepherd, and he will guide them to springs of living water; and God will wipe away every tear from their eyes.

Revelation 7:15–17

Prayer at the Death of a Little Child

Heavenly Father, Whose face the angels of little children do always behold, and Who by Thy Son Jesus Christ hast taught us that of such is the kingdom of heaven: we commend unto Thy faithful keeping this little child, number him (her) with the lambs in Thy bosom: that he (she) may dwell forever in Thy presence.   Amen.[1]

When the child can understand.   When a terminally sick child is sufficiently mature to understand, the pastor may comfort the little one with stanzas from familiar hymns, words from the Scriptures and prayers. Children also become apprehensive about death. Almost every child has seen adults weeping at the time of a death and heard an older person say, "He has gone to heaven," or "Now he is with the Lord." The anguish of the adults may cause the little one to fear death. In fact, many 6- to 9-year-olds are afraid of death when they get sick and talk about it with nurses in a hospital. The following stanzas may comfort a very sick child.

Jesus loves me, this I know,
For the Bible tells me so;
Little ones to Him belong;
They are weak, but He is strong.
Yes, Jesus loves me,
Yes Jesus loves me,
Yes Jesus loves me—
The Bible tells me so.

Anna B. Warner

I think when I read that sweet story of old,
When Jesus was here among men,

---

[1] Russell L. Dicks, *Comfort Ye My People* (New York: The Macmillan Co., 1947), p. 52.

How He called little children as lambs to His fold,
I should like to have been with Him then.

I wish that His hands had been placed on my head,
That His arms had been thrown around me,
And that I might have seen His kind look when He said,
"Let the little ones come unto Me."

Yet still to His footstool in prayer I may go,
And ask for a share of His love;
And if I thus earnestly seek Him below,
I shall see Him and hear Him above.

Jemima Thompson Luke

PRAYER WITH A DYING CHILD

Dear Lord Jesus, we love You
Because we know that You love us.
You take a little child kindly in Your arms
And You keep it warm and safe near Your heart.
You are always caring for us
To protect us from any harm,
So, we need never be afraid
For we can trust You always.
Bless us now with sleep and rest
And always keep us in your care.   Amen.

A PRAYER WITH LOVED ONES FOR A CHILD WHO IS DYING

Eternal God, who through Thy Son Jesus Christ has shown
a warm welcome to little children, help us to believe in this
hour of stress and strain that the everlasting arms of Thy
love are extended to him (her) who is critically sick. Enable
us to feel that he (she) is being lifted above the struggles
of this life, where there is no sorrow, or pain any more. We
thank Thee for the comforting knowledge of Thy house with
many rooms, knowing that if this were not so our Lord
would have told us. We praise Thee for all Thy goodness
and beseech Thee to strengthen us to the end, that we might
be faithful unto death and receive the crown of life. In
Jesus' Name.   Amen.

Friedrich Rest

The Death of a Youth

The will to live is usually very forceful in a young person. A terminally sick youth may not resign himself to thoughts about death until the very end, if at all.

In talking with a 20-year-old student nurse who was critically sick a month previously, I asked, "Did you think that you might die?"

Student nurse: No. I didn't think about that.

I: Try to recall carefully. Were you ever afraid that you might not recover?

Student nurse: I really didn't know how sick I was at the time, so it didn't enter my mind. I knew I was sick, but perhaps the sedation kept me semiconscious. No, I didn't think about death.

Conversing with a physically healthy 19-year-old girl from a religious family, I asked, "Do you, at any times, fear death?"

She: Yes, I do.

I: When do you usually think about that?

She: When I've done something wrong.

I: Like what?

She: Like sassing my parents or necking with my boy friend.

I: What do you think will cause you to die?

She: I know it sounds silly, but sometimes I worry about an infection.

I: What kind of an infection?

She: Like blood poisoning. And would you believe it? I caught my finger on the car door yesterday and hurt it. It would happen to me. Right here.

I: Did your finger bleed?

She: No—you can see—the skin was not broken. But later I worried about it.

I: I take it that this happened after you had done something "wrong." Is that it?

She: Yes, . . . that's it.

In one instance the girl might have died but she didn't think of death. The one who was physically healthy worried about it. Most healthy young people do fear death at times. The most prevalent phobias are cancer, heart diseases, leukemia and accidents.

When a young person realizes the seriousness of the affliction the pastor should be alert for signs of the fear of death. It may be said that every boy and girl has at some time been disobedient, or neglected religious practices, or experienced conflict with parents, or cursed, or harbored erotic thoughts or engaged in some forbidden activity. When there is nothing much other to do than to live with one's thoughts and endure sickness, any "wrong" activity may become the source of guilt and fear.

In ministering to a terminally sick youth the pastor ought to be alert for questions and statements such as: "Does God always forgive a person?"; "I know I should have listened to Mom; she didn't want me to get the motorcycle"; "I'm not afraid, Reverend, but does the devil torment people forever?" or "I know I'm going to get over this and be well again." If the patient becomes very religious, wants to read the Bible and talk about religion with the pastor, he may fear death.

It is important for the clergyman to have privacy when ministering to a dying youth, at least until he has had ample time to share any spiritual problems with him. When the patient does share misgivings about past conduct or harbors resentments against God, the understanding pastor may help the young person to an acceptance of God's love and care.

During prolonged illness, the pastor may suggest Holy Communion for the comfort and strengthening of the soul. It helps the parents if they participate in this sacrament with their child.

Reassurance for a dying youth. When the young person has been reared in a religious environment, the conscience may be more sensitive than when the youth has had little or no religious training. In ministering to a youth of the church, the clergyman may assume that the youth has thought about past sins even though he may not specifically have said so.

FROM THE SCRIPTURE

Search me, O God, and know my heart!
Try me and know my thoughts!
And see if there be any wicked way in me,
and lead me in the way everlasting!

Psalm 139:23–24

Help us, O God of our salvation,
for the glory of thy name;
deliver us, and forgive our sins,
for thy name's sake!

Psalm 79:9

Because, if you confess with your lips that Jesus is Lord and
believe in your heart that God raised him from the dead, you
will be saved. For man believes with his heart and so is
justified, and he confesses with his lips and so is saved. The
Scripture says, "No one who believes in him will be put to
shame."

Romans 10:9–11

How precious is thy steadfast love, O God!
The children of men take refuge in the shadow
of thy wings.
They feast on the abundance of thy house,
and thou givest them drink from the river
of thy delights.
For with thee is the fountain of life;
in thy light do we see light.

Psalm 36:7–9

". . . Be strong and of good courage; be not frightened,
neither be dismayed; for the Lord your God is with you
wherever you go."

Joshua 1:9

Prayer With a Youth Who Has Fears

Our dear Heavenly Father,
Thou hast blessed us in many ways

With food, shelter, and loved ones who care,
With friends to support us,
And the Church to guide us.
We have not always been obedient
And we sincerely regret our transgressions,
Knowing also that Thou dost understand
And love us just as we are.
We are particularly thankful for Jesus
Who in love suffered and died for us,
That we might have forgiveness.
And now, we pray Thee, dear Jesus,
Accept our heartfelt prayers;
Remove from our thoughts any fears
We harbor and comfort us with Thy Presence.
Help us to trust completely in Thee;
Assured that to them that love Thee
All things work together for good.   Amen.

Prayer With a Youth Without Fears

Dear God and Father, we love Thee;
We would praise Thee as we do a loved one
And say, "Blessed art Thou, O Lord our God."
For all the blessings of life, we thank Thee,
For our loved ones, the church and its message,
For our teachers, the doctor, nurses and our spiritual guidance,
For all who have helped us with their love and care
We sincerely thank Thee.
Now in this sickness be Thou ever near us,
Bless everything that is done in our behalf,
And in Thy good appointed time
Deliver us from all our distresses,
And we would praise Thee
Now and evermore.   Amen.

At the bedside of a deceased youth. The deceased
youth's family and friends usually appreciate the pastor's presence
at the bedside. In reverence, at the close of an earthly life, the
clergyman may offer a welcome suggestion when he says, "May

we now pause reverently and turn our thoughts to God in prayer?"

A Prayer at the Bedside of a Deceased Youth

Our heavenly Father, we pause in deep reverence
In Thy Holy Presence to pray,
That Thou wouldst accept unto Thyself
The soul of our loved one and grant to him (her)
The joy and peace in Thy heavenly home.
And grant, O Lord, that we may again be with him (her)
Who is with Thee,
And enjoy the eternal Kingdom
Forever and forever.   Amen.

When One Is Dying in Maturity

A mature person's attitude in terminal sickness depends upon a number of factors. The most important of these are the patient's beliefs, finances, dependent children, self-sufficiency of the spouse and the type of medication he is receiving.

As terminal patients, they may be classified in three categories: those who do not know it, those who know it but will not accept it, and those who are aware of it and will talk about it. To tell or not to tell the patient has been previously discussed. It remains for the pastor to minister to the parishioner in accordance with his attitude.

A middle-aged doctor was terminally sick with cancer and had previously experienced two operations. Surely he must have known that he was terminally sick. Yet, to the very end he did not talk about it to his pastor, but conversed in terms of getting better. However, he did dispose of some of his property to favored relatives and asked his pastor to bring him communion when the sacrament was observed in the church. The pastor could minister to him in terms of reassurance as he would to a parishioner who expressed his thoughts, but the doctor gave no indication that this man either feared death or anticipated it.

When there are feelings of guilt. In contrast, Mrs. J, a middle-aged woman with a daughter and son in high school, hesitated to express her thoughts at first. But one morning, when she was receiving cobalt treatments in the privacy of her hospital room, she said to her pastor, "It's no use pretending any longer. I know my days are numbered, Reverend, and I am concerned."

> Pastor: Would you share your concern with me?
>
> Mrs. J: We're a proud family, Reverend. I never wanted my children to associate with others who are not good enough.
>
> Pastor: Is that so?
>
> Mrs. J: I'm a selfish woman. I never wanted to share my husband or my children with other people, and I know that's not right.
>
> Pastor: What causes you to think that it isn't right?
>
> Mrs. J: Did I tell you about the vision I had?
>
> Pastor: No. I'd like to hear about it.
>
> Mrs. J: It wasn't a dream, Reverend. I wasn't asleep. I must have been in a coma. It was a vision . . . beautiful. I was walking with a basket of flowers on my arm, and I came to a river. I looked over and I could see people, I knew some of them; they were so happy and I thought, "That must be heaven." But I wouldn't dare tell whom I saw there because they might think they were going to die. I stood there and watched them and wished I were there. It was such a beautiful place, Reverend. My flowers had such a pleasant odor but each time I smelled them, one of the flowers wilted. I wanted to cross the river. Reverend, do you think that I'll get across the river?

The pastor noticed that each time she smelled a flower, it wilted. He asked, "Mrs. J what makes you have any doubt about it?"

She wasn't ready to share her guilt until two days later when he brought her Holy Communion after she requested it. Having spoken the words of the general confession in the ritual, she interrupted him saying, "Reverend I feel that the confession is not 'deep' enough." He urged her, "Won't you please tell me what is disturbing you, so you can find peace for your soul?"

Finally, she relieved her disturbed conscience by telling him that in the first year of marriage she had submitted to an abortion. It had plagued her conscience ever since. Thereafter, her pastor could help her accept God's forgiveness through her sincere repentance and faith in the Lord.

When a dying person expresses spiritual concern or tells of a vision, the pastor may be alert for strong feelings of guilt or inadequacy.

When one has no specific spiritual problems. In contrast to Mrs. J, Mr. K, 55, was a good father, served the church in various capacities, was a community leader and loved by his wife.

Their marriage was happy, even accepting the usual quarrels that ensue when two people live together for many years. They realized that no male or female fully appreciates or understands the physical, mental, emotional and spiritual needs of the other. With love and understanding, they accepted and respected each other. They were sufficiently intelligent to understand that words said in anger are usually regretted. They let time, understanding and love heal all wounds.

When a person has lived a life motivated predominantly by love and faith, there may be no regrets as death approaches. A widow said to me recently, "There wasn't a day in these later years that my husband and I didn't read a few verses from the Bible together. We had our differences like other people, but we loved each other. After the morning meal or in the evening, we had our devotions together. Then, we'd kiss each other and go about whatever we had planned."

Mr. K died of a heart ailment after a month's time. During

the sickness his pastor visited him regularly. There were no feelings of guilt and Mr. K always welcomed his pastor's call.

Reassurance for one dying in maturity. A hymn that may be particularly meaningful to a dying person was written about a 100 years ago. It is a testimony to the timelessness of faith.

> What a friend we have in Jesus,
>   All our sins and griefs to bear!
> What a privilege to carry
>   Everything to God in prayer!
> O what peace we often forfeit,
>   O what needless pain we bear,
> All because we do not carry
>   Everything to God in prayer!
>
> Have we trials and temptations?
>   Is there trouble anywhere?
> We should never be discouraged:
>   Take it to the Lord in prayer!
> Can we find a friend so faithful,
>   Who will all our sorrows share?
> Jesus knows our every weakness—
>   Take it to the Lord in prayer!
>
> Are we weak and heavy-laden,
>   Cumbered with a load of care?
> Precious Saviour, still our Refuge—
>   Take it to the Lord in prayer!
> Do thy friends despise, forsake Thee?
>   Take it to the Lord in prayer!
> In His arms He'll take and shield thee,
>   Thou wilt find a solace there.
>   *Joseph Scriven* (1820–1886)

Any or all of the following Scripture selections may be helpful to one who is dying in maturity.

> I lift up my eyes to the hills.
> From whence does my help come?
> My help comes from the Lord,
>   who made heaven and earth.

He will not let your foot be moved,
he who keeps you will not slumber.
Behold, he who keeps Israel
will neither slumber nor sleep.

The Lord is your keeper;
the Lord is your shade
on your right hand.
The sun shall not smite you by day,
nor the moon by night.

The Lord will keep you from all evil;
he will keep your life.
The Lord will keep
your going out and your coming in
from this time forth and for evermore.

Psalm 121

"The Lord is my portion," says my soul,
"therefore I will hope in him."
The Lord is good to those who wait for him,
to the soul that seeks him.
It is good that one should wait quietly
for the salvation of the Lord.

Lamentations 3:24–26

I have been young, and now am old;
yet I have not seen the righteous forsaken
or his children begging bread.

Psalm 37:25

"Truly, truly, I say to you, he who believes has eternal life.
I am the bread of life. . . . This is the bread which comes
down from heaven, that a man may eat of it and not die.
I am the living bread which came down from heaven; if any
man eats of this bread, he will live for ever; and the bread
which I shall give for the life of the world is my flesh."

John 6:47–48, 50–51

For whatever is born of God overcomes the world; and this is
the victory that overcomes the world, our faith. Who is it
that overcomes the world but he who believes that Jesus is

the Son of God? . . . And this is the testimony, that God gave us eternal life, and this life is in his Son. He who has the Son has life; he who has not the Son has not life.

I John 5:4–5, 11–12

"I have said this to you, that in me you may have peace. In the world you have tribulation; but be of good cheer, I have overcome the world."

John 16:33

Prayer With a Mature Person

O Lord, our God, through Thy blessed Son
Thou hast invited all who labor
And are heavy-laden to come to Thee.
We, therefore, approach Thy throne of grace in prayer.
O Thou Lamb of God who takest away
The sins of the world, have mercy upon us!
With Thy suffering Thou hast borne our sins
And carried our sorrows.
Visit us with Thy salvation,
Cleanse us from all our sins,
Deliver us from suffering,
Grant Thy healing forces in body and soul
In Thy good appointed time
Deliver us from all evil
And receive us into glory everlasting;
Where with all the angels and the saints
We shall praise Thy holy name forever.   Amen.

A Psalm Prayer

Incline thy ear, O Lord, and answer me,
for I am poor and needy.
Preserve my life, for I am godly;
save thy servant who trusts in thee.
Thou are my God; be gracious to me, O Lord,
for to thee do I cry all the day.
Gladden the soul of thy servant,
for to thee, O Lord, do I lift up my soul.
For thou, O Lord, are good and forgiving,

abounding in steadfast love to all who call on thee.
Give ear, O Lord, to my prayer;
hearken to my cry of supplication.
In the day of my trouble I call on thee,
for thou dost answer me.

Psalm 86:1–7

ROMAN CATHOLIC PRIESTLY PRAYER

THE RECOMMENDATION OF A DEPARTING SOUL

Let us pray.[2]

We commend to Thee, O Lord, the soul of this Thy servant
. . . N . . . and beseech Thee, O Jesus Christ, Redeemer
of the world! that, as in Thy mercy to him (her) Thou
becamest Man, so now Thou wouldst vouchsafe to admit
him (her) into the number of the blessed. Remember, O
Lord, that he (she) is Thy creature, not made by strange
gods, but by Thee, the only true and living God; for there
is no other God but Thee, and none can work Thy wonders.
Let his (her) soul find comfort in Thy sight, and remember
not his (her) former sins, nor any of those excesses which he
(she) has fallen into, through the violence of passion and
corruption. For although he (she) has sinned, yet he (she)
has still retained a true faith in Thee, Father, Son, and Holy
Ghost; he (she) has had a zeal for Thy honor, and faith-
fully adored Thee, his (her) God, and the Creator of all
things.

May the most tender Virgin Mary, Mother of God, the
kindest comforter of those that mourn, commend the soul
of . N . . ., her servant, to her Son, that through her
motherly intervention he (she) may not fear the terrors of
death, but may with her help, in gladness reach the desire
of his (her) heart, and dwelling-place in our heavenly
country.   Amen.

---

2 *Sick Call Ritual,* Compiled from The Vatican Typical Edition (New
York, Boston, Cincinnati, Chicago, San Francisco: Benziger Brothers, Inc.,
1947), pp. 70, 71, 73.

At the Last Moment[3]

Such words as the following are again and again to be repeated in his ear:

Into Thy hands, O Lord, I commend my spirit.
O Lord Jesus Christ, receive my spirit.
Holy Mary, pray for me.
Mary Mother of grace, Mother of mercy, do thou
    protect me from the enemy, and receive me at
    the hour of death.
St. Joseph, pray for me.
St. Joseph, in company with thy Spouse, the
    Blessed Virgin, open to me the bosom of divine mercy.
Jesus, Mary, Joseph, I give you my heart and
    my soul;
Jesus, Mary, Joseph, assist me in my last agony;
Jesus, Mary, Joseph, may I enter with
    you into peace and rest at last.

After the soul has departed the priest will say a responsory, finally commending the soul to God.

A Prayer After a Faithful Believer Has Deceased[4]

Remember, O Lord, Thy servant (name) according to the favor Thou bearest unto Thy people, and grant that, increasing in knowledge and love of Thee, he (she) may go from strength to strength in the life of perfect service in Thy heavenly kingdom; through Jesus Christ our Lord, who liveth and reigneth with Thee and the Holy Ghost, ever one God, world without end.   Amen.

An Aging Person

Clergymen minister to more people over 65 than any other group. An aging person's attitude toward approaching death is influenced by the patient's beliefs, how much satisfaction has

---

[3] *Ibid.*, pp. 90, 91.
[4] An ancient prayer, source unknown.

been derived from life, how one has lived, his physical condition, dependency of the patient upon others, loneliness and if he has dependents.

Not all old people look forward to death with anticipation. The will to live is very strong. If the individual is fairly comfortable, surrounded with loving care and feels needed, there will be reluctance on the part of the old person to accept the possibility of death. This may be evidenced by the acquisition of new clothes or other material things by a person in advanced old age.

Recall that in Chapter One, philosophies of death and immortality were discussed. Most people of advanced age realize that the end of earthly life is inevitable. They know the average length of the life span and the Scriptural observation, . . . "or even by reason of strength fourscore" (Psalm 90:10). Consequently when people reach the 70's and 80's, most of them realize that there are not many years left.

When an old person anticipates death. When an old person says, "I wish the Lord would take me home," the clergyman may accept the statement as sincere. When the individual has strong beliefs in immortality, and has lived a life of faith, there may be a longing for release from "the burden of the flesh."

Beliefs play a most important role in this attitude. Many old people look forward to a reunion with loved ones and friends who have passed on, especially if they have outlived a child or children. Those who have lived in accordance with their religious beliefs and practices may anticipate "reward" in the eternal life. They may not be able to pinpoint or identify the nature of the rewards, but they are certain that God will give them eternal happiness or bliss. In other instances, aged persons may anticipate death because they feel they are a burden on the family. Unfortunately, in many instances, they are.

Mr. L, 84, often expressed his wish to die to the nurses. He was dismissed from the hospital by his doctor. For three consecutive days he waited for his son to come to take him home. When the son finally arrived, his wife refused to enter the room or to speak to the old man. She undoubtedly let him know that "he was in the way" and not welcome in their home.

Old people may become very lonely, for they have little in common with the younger generation. Most of their friends have deceased. The loneliness is even greater when the old person has been taken into an unfamiliar environment. As the old parishioner grows weaker, the pastor's calls will be all the more appreciated, although he must not expect an old person to thank him or express gratitude. Some of them will do it, but most will not. Perhaps they are just too weary to say "Thank you" or "Please come again."

Reassurances for an aged person.   A clergyman may call many times upon an aged and dying parishioner. He may be helpful by taking the time on each call to listen to what the dying one has to say. He must exercise patience for he may hear the same story time and again. With understanding, he may assume that if the Lord lets him live that long, he, too, will someday appreciate the kindness and the understanding of another clergyman.

The old person will be helped if the pastor will read from the Scripture or quote familiar hymns and offer prayers.

SCRIPTURE SELECTIONS FOR AN ELDERLY WOMAN BELIEVER

The Lord is merciful and gracious,
 slow to anger and abounding in steadfast love.
He will not always chide,
 nor will he keep his anger for ever.
He does not deal with us according to our sins,
 nor requite us according to our iniquities.
For as the heavens are high above the earth,
 so great is his steadfast love toward those who
  fear him;
as far as the east is from the west,
 so far does he remove our transgressions from us.

          Psalm 103:8–12

A good wife who can find?
 She is far more precious than jewels.

The heart of her husband trusts in her,
and he will have no lack of gain.
She does him good, and not harm,
all the days of her life.

She opens her hand to the poor,
and reaches out her hands to the needy.

Strength and dignity are her clothing,
and she laughs at the time to come.
She opens her mouth with wisdom,
and the teaching of kindness is on her tongue.
She looks well to the ways of her household,
and does not eat the bread of idleness.
Her children rise up and call her blessed;
her husband also, and he praises her:
"Many women have done excellently,
but you surpass them all."
Charm is deceitful, and beauty is vain,
but a woman who fears the Lord is to be praised.
Give her of the fruit of her hands,
and let her works praise her in the gates.

Proverbs 31:10–12, 20, 25–31

But Jesus, aware of this, said to them, "Why do you trouble the woman? For she has done a beautiful thing to me. For you always have the poor with you, but you will not always have me. In pouring this ointment on my body she has done it to prepare me for burial. Truly, I say to you, wherever this gospel is preached in the whole world, what she has done will be told in memory of her."

Matthew 26:10–13

Now there was at Joppa a disciple named Tabitha, which means Dorcas or Gazelle. She was full of good works and acts of charity. In those days she fell sick and died; and when they had washed her, they laid her in an upper room. Since Lydda was near Joppa, the disciples, hearing that Peter was there, sent two men to him entreating him, "Please come to us without delay." So Peter rose and went with them. And when he had come, they took him to the upper room. All the widows stood beside him weeping, and showing coats and garments which Dorcas made while she was with them. But Peter put them all outside and knelt down and prayed; then turning to the body he said, "Tabitha, rise." And she opened her eyes, and when she saw Peter she sat up. And he gave her his hand and lifted her up. Then calling the saints and widows he presented her alive. And it became known throughout all Joppa, and many believed in the Lord.

Acts 9:36–42

For this reason I bow my knees before the Father, from whom every family in heaven and on earth is named, that according to the riches of his glory he may grant you to be strengthened with might through his Spirit in the inner man, and that Christ may dwell in your hearts through faith; that you, being rooted and grounded in love, may have power to comprehend with all the saints what is the breadth and length and height and depth, and to know the love of Christ which surpasses knowledge, that you may be filled with all the fullness of God.

Ephesians 3:14–19

SCRIPTURE SELECTIONS FOR AN ELDERLY MAN

Blessed is the man
    who walks not in the counsel of the wicked,
nor stands in the way of sinners,
    nor sits in the seat of scoffers;
but his delight is in the law of the Lord,
    and on his law he meditates day and night.
He is like a tree
    planted by streams of water,
that yields its fruit in its season,
    and its leaf does not wither.
In all that he does, he prospers.

The wicked are not so,
    but are like chaff which the wind drives away.

Therefore the wicked will not stand in the judgment,
    nor sinners in the congregation of the righteous;
for the Lord knows the way of the righteous,
    but the way of the wicked will perish.

Psalm 1

God is our refuge and strength,
    a very present help in trouble.
Therefore we will not fear though the earth should change,
    though the mountains shake in the heart of the sea;
though its waters roar and foam,
    though the mountains tremble with its tumult.

Psalm 46:1–3

Then the King will say to those at his right hand, "Come, O blessed of my Father, inherit the kingdom prepared for you from the foundation of the world; for I was hungry and you gave me food, I was thirsty and you gave me drink, I was a stranger and you welcomed me, I was naked and you clothed me, I sick and you visited me, I was in prison and you came to me."

Then the righteous will answer him, "Lord, when did we see thee hungry and feed thee, or thirsty and give thee drink? And when did we see thee a stranger and welcome thee, or naked and clothe thee? And when did we see thee sick or in prison and visit thee?" And the King will answer them, "Truly, I say to you, as you did it to one of the least of these my brethren, you did it to me."

Matthew 25:34–40

But our commonwealth is in heaven, and from it we await a Savior, the Lord Jesus Christ, who will change our lowly body to be like his glorious body, by the power which enables him even to subject all things to himself.

Philippians 3:20–21

After this I looked, and behold, a great multitude which no man could number, from every nation, from all tribes and peoples and tongues, standing before the throne and before the Lamb, clothed in white robes, with palm branches in their hands, and crying out with a loud voice, "Salvation belongs to our God who sits upon the throne, and to the Lamb!" And all the angels stood round the throne and round the elders and the four living creatures, and they fell on their faces before the throne and worshiped God, saying, "Amen! Blessing and glory and wisdom and thanksgiving and honor and power and might be to our God for ever and ever! Amen."

Therefore are they before the throne of God, and serve him day and night within his temple; and he who sits upon the throne will shelter them with his presence.

They shall hunger no more, neither thirst any more; the sun shall not strike them, nor any scorching heat. For the Lamb in the midst of the throne will be their shepherd, and he will guide them to springs of living water; and God will wipe away every tear from their eyes.

Revelation 7:9–12, 15–17

Older people usually find comfort in familiar hymns that express their religious thoughts. The following titles suggest some of them that the pastor may use.

"O Love That Wilt Not Let Me Go," by George Matheson
"For All the Saints Who From Their Labors Rest," by W. W. How
"Jesus, Saviour, Pilot Me," by Edward Hopper
"Still, Still With Thee," by Harriet Beecher Stowe
"What a Friend We Have in Jesus," by Joseph Scriven
"In Heavenly Love Abiding," by Anna Laetitia Waring

PRAYER WITH AN ELDERLY PERSON

Dear God, our Heavenly Father,
Thou has assured us in Thy Word
That though the mountains should depart
And the hills be removed,
Thy kindness shall not depart from us,
Nor Thy mercy and providential care.

Most faithful Father, we did often forget Thee,
Yet, Thou didst never forget us,
But didst receive us anew
Each time we called upon Thee.
Comfort us with the assurance
That in sickness or distress we are Thine;
Through Jesus, Thou didst call us
Into the family of the saints.
Grant us steadfast faith and love
And be our comfort in life and in death,
Through Jesus Christ, our Saviour.   Amen.

A Prayer for an Elderly Person

Our blessed Lord, Thou hast invited all to come
Unto Thee who are weak and heavy-laden;
For Thou wilt give rest unto the weary soul.
We come to Thee in our prayers
In behalf of our loved one
Whose earthly tenure is drawing to a close.
Thou Lamb of God hast borne and taken away
The sins of the world.
Visit this Thy child, with Thy salvation.
Deliver him (her) according to Thy will
That he (she) may come home to Thee
As a sheaf of ripened grain
Comes in in its season.
Accept him (her) unto Thyself,
That he (she) may rejoice in Thy Presence
Forever and forever.   Amen.

A Prayer With an Elderly Person Who Is Dying[5]

Almighty and merciful God and Father! My life draws to a
close. Thou are calling me from this earth. Thy will be done.
I place myself in Thy hands and rest in Thine eternal love.
Graciously didst Thou lead me hitherto. Oh, mercifully
conduct me to the heavenly mansions of peace and life

---

[5] H. J. Schick, *Pastor's Pocket Manual* (St. Louis: Eden Publishing
House, 1930), p. 87.

eternal. Count not my sins against me; let grace prevail over justice. Grant me pardon and the crown of life for Jesus' sake. Come, heavenly Father; come Divine Redeemer; come Holy Spirit! I am Thine! Into Thy hands I commend my spirit.   Amen.

CHAPTER SIX

PREPARING A CONGREGATION
For The PASTOR'S MINISTRY
To DYING PERSONS

Of the millions of people who are active church members, there are many who know very little about the pastor's responsibilities. They do know that he conducts the weekly services, administers the sacraments, perhaps teaches a class and officiates at funerals and weddings.

On the occasion of an annual meeting of the congregation, he may report the number of pastoral calls during the previous year; but he could scarcely take enough time to explain why he made all those visits. Perhaps there is no phase of the minister's work that consumes more of his time, prayers, thoughts and preparation than his pastoral care. Yet, the pastoral office is far less understood than his priestly and prophetic responsibilities.

Pastoral calls may be social, evangelistic, educational, family or marriage counseling, informative, enlisting or spiritually supporting, such as a call upon the sick and dying.

From the Pulpit

The clergyman does not hesitate to devote one or more sermons each year to stewardship, or missions, or religious education and other important functions of the church in which he is directly involved. But, he may seldom preach about the pastoral office and the purposes of the pastoral sick call.

In many denominations a memorial Sunday is observed each year when the names of the departed members are mentioned and their memory honored. Many of the bereaved purposely stay away from this service because they are sensitive about their loved

121

ones and they fear that the pastor's message will be morbid or play with their emotions.

This service is a chance for the minister to tell his people about the Scriptural implications regarding immortality and man's preparation for the eternal life. It affords him an opportunity to share the significance of the sick call, and to renew understanding of how our religious virtues may help us meet our spiritual needs in time of sickness and death.

He may use the Scripture to confirm the believer's faith in God and thus regard death as a triumph rather than a defeat. He may explain how he may help the dying person use whatever spiritual resources he may have to meet his needs in life as well as in death.

In these sermons the pastor must be careful never to reveal anything of a confidential nature that has been shared with him by members of the congregation. Examples from experiences in previous congregations, from this book or from Holy Scripture will serve his purposes. He may mention that he sacredly regards anything that is shared with him in confidence. However, it should be emphasized that he must never violate that principle of ethics even in private conversations!

From the pulpit, the pastor may remotely prepare his people to use the pastoral call to their fullest advantage. He may help his people, through preaching, to understand the essential preparations for the final moments of earthly life in order that they may be triumphant.

In Classes

From time to time the minister is asked to address various church classes and organizations. These are also opportunities to explain the significance of the pastoral sick call. The Roman Catholic priest's mission in the sickroom is well defined by his church, but Protestant and Jewish clergymen must rely mostly upon their own spiritual intuition or divine guidance.

To this writer's knowledge there is no textbook written by a competent theologian to help laymen understand the significance of the pastoral office, particularly in regard to ministering to the dying. The Roman Catholic Church has its detailed Catechism to help priests instruct their people. Little is left unsaid in regard to preparation for the eternal life. Some Protestant catechisms contain sections that specifically state the basic requirements for eternal salvation. Apart from such sources, Protestant and Jewish clergymen may need to devise their own courses of study.

Pastoral Letters

Pastoral letters, written by the minister from time to time, are instructive and express his love and concern for his people. The weekly bulletin will scarcely serve that purpose because it is too impersonal.

Christmas is not the wisest time to send this message. In most instances it gets lost and forgotten in the confusion. Less hectic times of the year, such as October or May, are more opportune. The clergyman may prepare his people for it from the lectern or in the Sunday bulletin. It should be printed professionally and sent by first class mail. There should be nothing cheap about it!

A PASTORAL LETTER CONCERNING THE SICK CALL

(The name and address should be typed and the letter signed personally.)

Beloved in the Lord: or
Dear Christian Friend: or
Dear Friend:

In pursuit of my calling as your pastor, I take this means to communicate with you regarding a spiritual matter of deep concern. It has to do with the spiritual ministry to you at the time of sickness and approaching death.

Do not worry about what I will say to you at such a time. What you say to me is infinitely more important. And whatever you share with me is in strictest confidence. Sharing deep feelings in times of crisis is a Christian right.

Your pastor considers it a privilege to minister and assist

you in your faith. God's Word speaks to all our needs. Through repentance, faith and prayer we may approach our God and Saviour who will confirm the spiritual strength and comfort the soul.

When you are sick, worried, afraid, or harbor feelings of fear or guilt, God opens the way, through His grace, to that peace that passes understanding.

With humility I come to you as your pastor, for the sake of our Lord, particularly at the time of severe sickness or when the earthly pilgrimage may draw to a close.

When you or your loved ones desire spiritual assistance, I will appreciate it if you will inform me.

May God bless you,

Sincerely,
(*Signature*)

The Bulletin or Church Paper

The minister may use the weekly or monthly church paper or bulletin to instruct his people regarding the pastoral call. He may make it a point to help his people understand the various missions of the pastoral call.

A series of brief articles or paragraphs in the bulletin or church paper may not only be instructive but may help the pastor attain his objective in making the call.

CHAPTER SEVEN

SACRAMENTS,
RITES For The DYING

Holy Communion

Many Protestants request Holy Communion when death is approaching. They regard it as an efficacious last rite and as an important final preparation for the eternal life. As with Extreme Unction, Holy Communion may strengthen the soul for life either in this world or in heaven. Many observe it also for its spiritual healing qualities.

Most Protestant Holy Communion rituals for the sick are too long to be practical when a person is dying or in a semiconscious condition. Many old people cannot focus their attention for a long period of time. When time is of essence, the clergyman may abbreviate the ritual to meet the need.

It is commonly accepted that the ritual should include, in brief form, an exhortation, a confession, an absolution, the words of institution, partaking of the elements and a closing prayer and benediction.

Whenever possible, loved ones should participate in the sacrament for the comfort of their souls. However, the pastor must not withhold the sacrament for the convenience of a spouse or another relative or friend who is not present when the patient desires Holy Communion.

In a Hospital

Observing the sacrament in a home rarely poses a problem for the pastor because he will be assured of privacy. In a hospital, after identifying himself with the head nurse, he may tell her the purpose of his call. She will arrange for him to have privacy with the patient without interruptions. When his call is completed he must remember to inform her in order that any ministrations to the patient may be resumed.

The Roman Catholic priest usually communicates his patient prior to breakfast.

A Brief Communion Service for the Dying

Exhortation

Dearly Beloved in the Lord; since, in the providence of God you are not able to receive Holy Communion in the church and you desire the sacrament to strengthen your soul, express your fellowship with the saints, and your love for the Lord, I invite you to approach with me now to the throne of grace and make your humble confession to Almighty God.

Confession

Almighty and most merciful God our heavenly Father; we humble ourselves before Thee. We have grievously sinned against Thee in thought, in word, and in deed. We have broken Thy commandments and turned aside every one of us from the way of life. Yet, now, O most merciful Father, hear us when we call upon Thee with penitent hearts and for the sake of Jesus our Saviour have mercy upon us. Pardon our sins and take away our guilt. Purify us by the inspiration of Thy Holy Spirit, and make us worthy to serve Thee now and in eternity.   Amen.

Absolution

Upon this humble confession which you have made, as a minister of our Lord Jesus Christ, I declare unto you who do truly repent and heartily believe, the forgiveness of all your sins in the name of the Father and of the Son and of the Holy Spirit.

Words of Institution

The Lord Jesus in the same night in which He was betrayed, took bread; and when he had given thanks, He brake it, and said, "Take, eat, this is my Body which is broken for you;

this do in remembrance of Me." After the same manner also, he took the cup, when he had supped, saying, "This cup is the New Testament in my Blood; this do ye as oft as ye drink it, in remembrance of Me."

THE COMMUNION

Take and eat: This is the Body of our Lord Jesus Christ, which was broken for you. Do this in remembrance of Him. Take and drink: This Cup is the New Testament in His Blood which was shed for you for the remission of sins. Do this in remembrance of Him. May this strengthen and preserve your soul into everlasting life.

PRAYER OF THANKSGIVING

We thank Thee, Our Lord, for Thy great mercy given to us in this Sacrament. So enrich us by Thy Holy Spirit that the life of Jesus may be made manifest in our mortal body, and all our days may be spent in Thy love and service.

THE LORD'S PRAYER

THE BENEDICTION

The grace of the Lord Jesus Christ, and the love of God, and the communion of the Holy Spirit, be with you.   Amen.

After the Communion Service the pastor may quietly replace the utensils in the kit and leave the room without further conversation except a brief farewell.

A Very Brief Communion Service

In the Name of the Father, and of the Son, and of the Holy Spirit.   Amen.

Our blessed Lord has invited us, "Come to me, all who labor and are heavy-laden, and I will give you rest." Thus our Saviour invites us to come to Him in repentance and faith and assures us His forgiveness and the blessing of eternal life.

The Lord Jesus, the same night in which He was betrayed, took bread; and when He had given thanks, he brake it, and said, "Take, eat, this is my Body which is broken for you; this do in remembrance of me."

(The patient may be given the sacred element.)

After the same manner also, He took the cup, when He had supped, saying, "This cup is the New Testament in My Blood; this do ye, as oft as ye drink it, in remembrance of Me."

(The patient may partake of the cup.)

May this strengthen and preserve your soul unto eternal life.

PRAYER AND BENEDICTION

Almighty God, so enrich us by Thy Holy Spirit that the life of Jesus may be made manifest in us, and all our days may be spent in Thy love and service, now and evermore, through Jesus Christ, our Redeemer.

The grace of our Lord Jesus Christ, and the love of God, and the communion of the Holy Spirit, be with you.   Amen.

Emergency Baptism[1]

Our Lord Jesus Christ has promised in His Word to grant forgiveness of sins and the gift of the Holy Spirit unto all who repent and turn to Him.

Do you solemnly consecrate yourself forever to the Lord Jesus Christ and do you promise in His strength to lead a sober, righteous and godly life? Do you desire now the sacrament of Holy Baptism?

(The patient may indicate the desire by word or facial expression.)

I baptize thee in the Name of the Father, and of the Son, and of the Holy Ghost.

---

[1] From *Book of Worship*, approved by the General Synod of the Evangelical and Reformed Church, 1947.

(If the minister is in reasonable doubt whether the person has been previously baptized he may use the following words at the application of the water: If thou art not already baptized, I baptize thee in the Name of the Father, and of the Son, and of the Holy Ghost.)

THE BLESSING

The very God of peace sanctify you wholly; and I pray God your whole spirit, and soul, and body, be preserved blameless unto the coming of our Lord Jesus Christ.   Amen.

A Brief Service of Anointing[2]

INTRODUCTION

When any person shall in humble faith desire the ministry of healing through Anointing or Laying on of Hands, the Minister may use such portion of the forgoing Office as he shall think fit [The "forgoing Office" contains prayers for healing, when there is small hope for recovery, when despondent, a commendatory prayer and a litany for the dying.] and the following:

ADMINISTRATION OF UNCTION

O Blessed Redeemer, relieve, we beseech Thee, by Thy indwelling power, the distress of this Thy servant; release him (her) from sin, drive away all pain of soul and body, that being restored to soundness of health, he may offer Thee praise and thanksgiving; who livest and reignest with the Father and the Holy Ghost, one God, world without end.   Amen.

I anoint thee with oil (or I lay my hand upon thee), in the Name of the Father, and of the Son, and of the Holy Ghost; beseeching the mercy of our Lord Jesus Christ, that all thy pain and sickness of body being put to flight, the blessing of health may be restored unto thee.   Amen.

---

[2] *The Book of Common Prayer* (New York: Morehouse Publishing Co.), p. 320.

Commendations of the Dying

Depart, O Christian Soul, out of this world. May God the Father Almighty, who created thee; and Jesus Christ, the Son of the Living God, who redeemed thee; and the Holy Spirit, who sanctified thee, preserve thy going out and thy coming in, from this time forth, even for evermore.

Amen.

Into thy hands, O merciful Saviour, we commend the soul of Thy servant, now departed from the body. Acknowledge, we humbly beseech Thee, a sheep of Thine own fold, a lamb of Thine own flock, a sinner of Thine own redeeming. Receive him (her) into the arms of Thy mercy, into the blessed rest of everlasting peace, and unto the glorious company of the saints in light.   Amen.

Into Thy care and keeping, O Lord, we commend the soul of our loved one and pray that Thou wouldst grant unto him (her) all the blessings of the eternal life that Thou hast ordained for Thy children from the beginning of time. Look with tender love upon the members of this bereaved household and grant them the guidance and comfort of Thy Holy Spirit, through Jesus Christ, our Saviour.   Amen.

And now may the grace of our Lord Jesus Christ the love of God the Father, and the communion of the Holy Spirit abide with you, now and evermore.   Amen.

APPENDIX

Ancient Egyptian Concepts of Death and Immortality

Man's belief in the hereafter dates as far back as recorded history.

Before the Children of Israel migrated to Egypt, the people there already had a philosophy of death that included ideas about immortality. At first, life beyond the grave was restricted for those of high social status—those people who made outstanding contributions to their civilization, amassed wealth and were moral according to their standards of morality. Their theologians might have concluded that the masses, who couldn't achieve much in this world, should have a better chance in the next one. At least they were given a way out of their struggles and suppression through eternal oblivion.

As time passed, ordinary people were also granted a type of immortality in that each identified himself with Osiris and hoped to live in the skies.

Ancient Egyptians also expressed their feelings of immortality in religious ceremonies. Oehler, an eminent authority on Old Testament theology, states that there is no trace in the Old Testament of the Egyptian notion that a continual connection subsists between the soul and the body after death. At the same time he states that the Roman historian Tacitus ascribed this conception to the Jews.[1]

The ancient Egyptians worshipped many gods, especially Osiris, king of the dead, who influenced his people through the funeral cult. His brother, Seth, who conspired against him, was

[1] See Oehler, *op. cit.*, p. 169.

regarded as the source of all evil. Osiris and his wife, Isis, had a son, Horus, who grew up to be Osiris remanifested.[2]

The legend states that Seth invited Osiris to a banquet with 72 fellow conspirators. Here they forced him into a coffin, shut the lid and threw it into the Nile. Isis recovered his body and brought it back to Egypt. Another time, when she was visiting Horus, Seth overcame Osiris once more, cut his body into fourteen pieces and hid them in various places in Egypt. Isis finally found all the pieces, joined them together with her magical powers, and Osiris came to life again. Thereafter, Osiris reigned as the king of the dead in the nether region.

This legend found expression in temple rites and on the feast day of Osiris in Abydos, when a drama was enacted depicting episodes in his life, particularly the final triumph. An image of the god was carried in a procession in a boat with curtains. At an appropriate time the curtain was drawn revealing the god. When the awestruck people saw the image, ecstatic shouting and dancing ensued.

There were many beliefs concerning life and death. It was difficult for the Egyptians to think of life except in conjunction with the body. Since they believed that the body would be resuscitated after death, the utmost care was taken to preserve it. Hence, those who could afford to do so, made arrangements for embalming. Elaborate tombs were constructed and the corpse was treated with natron and asphalt and wound in linen. The face mask was in linen and stucco. Many rites were observed in the process and at certain intervals the priest intoned magical words to assure the life of the body. Finally, it was placed on its side, as if in sleep, in a coffin.

Utensils, furniture, weapons, mirrors and other useful objects were placed in the tomb. Later, small models of the mummy were also placed in the tomb so that, when the owner was called upon to do a task that he did not like, one of the models could do it for him.

In a later period, the home of the dead was heaven, con·

---

2 *The Encyclopaedia Britannica*, 11th Ed. (New York), IX, 54.

sidered to be a very fertile region abounding in fruit and corn. It was called Sokhet Earu or "Field of Reeds,"[3] and every Egyptian had a chance to dwell there. However, the individual's life after death was contingent upon his morality in this world moreso than upon his wealth and position.

These concepts of death and immortality were prevalent when the Hebrew people dwelt in Egypt, and may have influenced Hebrew thought, contrary to Oehler's conclusion. It may be said, too, that God's revelation of Himself was not confined solely to the Hebrew people. God's plan of redemption and salvation is inherent in man's spiritual nature. It may have found expression in the legend of Osiris, as it did in various symbols of the Old Testament.

Ancient Roman Beliefs

During Jesus' time and before, Roman and Greek philosophers expressed conflicting views to the Egyptians' concept of immortality. People became more pessimistic; happiness was no longer the goal of philosophy.[4] If happiness could not be found in this life, man looked for it in the next one. The concept of another world was one of shadows, a gloomy, joyless, lower world. Homer's Ulysses saw the dead as shadows who greedily drank blood which gave them real life for a brief time. Though men longed for happiness in the hereafter, they shuddered at the thought of another world. The descent to Hades was regarded as full of horror.

As time passed and life in this world became more hopeless and oppressive, this view of immortality slowly changed. Joy in existence, in the beauty of the earth and of human life disappeared. The limitations of human nature and a sense of the vanity of all earthly things increased.

Death, once feared, became extolled as an emancipation.

---

[3] *Ibid.*, p. 55.

[4] Dr. Gerhard Uhlhorn, Abbot of Loccum and member of Supreme Consistory in Hanover, *The Conflict of Christianity with Heathenism* (New York: Charles Scribner's Sons, 1888), p. 73.

Cicero wrote, "After death we shall for the first time truly live." Seneca regarded the body as the urn for the Spirit and the other world as its real home.

In contrast to this view Caesar once said in the Senate, "Beyond this life there is no place for either trouble or joy," and Cato approvingly responded, "Beautifully and excellently has Caius Caesar spoken in this assembly concerning life and death, esteeming as false those things which are related of the lower world."[5]

Others believed as Caius Caesar and Cato. Pliny expressed it thus: "What folly it is to renew life after death! Where shall created beings find rest if you suppose that the shades in hell, and souls in heaven, continue to have any feelings? You rob us of man's greatest good, death. Let us rather find in the tranquility which preceded our existence, the pledge of the repose which is to follow it."[6]

At the time of Christ's advent these conflicting views of death and immortality were prevalent in the Roman culture that dominated the western civilization and were felt in Jerusalem through the influence of the Herods and the Roman and Greek philosophers.

Roman and Greek religious thought expressed the feeling that man's soul is immortal. In addition, in Roman theology there developed a consciousness of sin. Seneca discoursed on the depravity of man: "We have all sinned, some grievously, others more lightly, some purposely, others accidentally impelled or led astray; and not only have we transgressed, we shall continue to do so until the end of life."[7]

The Roman gods offered no help for this deep need for redemption. Under emperors such as Caligula and Nero, property, pleasure and life itself became insecure. While many would have welcomed death as a relief, there was no definite assurance that even death itself would offer the peace and security that men sought.

---

[5] *Ibid.,* p. 75.
[6] Pliny's Natural History, 7:55 from *ibid.,* p. 75.
[7] *Ibid.,* p. 77.

Amidst this uncertainty Roman philosophers turned to the orient for gods whose priesthood could reconcile man with the deity. In Roman religious rites the priest was nothing more than a master of ceremonies. There were no expiations and there was no desire to approach the gods. Men observed their duties toward the gods by performance of prescribed rites and offered the incense or sacrifice thinking or hoping that this would assure them some measure of protection in this world. But beyond that their gods offered no help.

When Jesus preached the message of redemption and eternal life, the eyes of many Roman and Greek philosophers were already turned to the Orient seeking the answer to their quest. The Apostle John, acquainted with the quest of Greek philosophy, offered the answer to it in the Prologue of his Gospel.

SCRIPTURE INDEX

INDEX